Remember and Give Thanks

Remember and Give Thanks

reflections on eucharist

Patrick McGoldrick

VERITAS

First published 2021 by
Veritas Publications
7–8 Lower Abbey Street
Dublin 1
Ireland
publications@veritas.ie
www.veritas.ie

ISBN 978 1 80097 012 0

10 9 8 7 6 5 4 3 2 1

A catalogue record for this book is available from the British Library.

Design & typesetting by Colette Dower, Veritas Publications
Printed in the Republic of Ireland by SPRINT-print, Dublin

Veritas books are printed on paper made from the wood pulp of managed forests. For every tree felled, at least one tree is planted, thereby renewing natural resources.

Contents

eucharist ... in celebration

already – not yet

Foreword

Patrick Jones

Father Patrick McGoldrick, priest of the Diocese of Derry, Professor Emeritus of Liturgy, St Patrick's College, Maynooth, died on 16 December 2020, aged eighty-three. *Ar dheis Dé go raibh a anam dílis.*

After ordination on 17 June 1962, he spent thirty-six years in the study and teaching of liturgy. After retiring as Professor of Liturgy at St Patrick's College, Maynooth, he was curate in the parish of Moville, Co. Donegal for twenty-two years.

Always Patrick to his family, his sister Caitríona and brothers Brian and Neil, both priests of the Diocese of Derry, mourn his loss. They are joined by many, especially colleagues in liturgy, students and staff of Maynooth College and parishioners of Moville, Co. Donegal.

Paddy was born in Buncrana, Co. Donegal on 12 August 1937, the eldest son of Liam and Kathleen McGoldrick. Following his secondary school education, he studied at St Patrick's College, Maynooth, taking a BA degree in classics and BD in theology before further studies for a licentiate and doctorate in theology. Ordained priest on 17 June 1962, his academic abilities, especially in dogmatic theology and ecclesiastical Latin, were well attested in his post-graduate years in the Dunboyne Establishment of Maynooth College. His thesis for the degree of DD, conferred by the Pontifical University in 1964, was on the theology of St Augustine. Paddy retained a high regard for Augustine and his writings. Paddy returned to the Diocese of Derry and was a member of the teaching staff of St Columb's College in Derry, 1964–5.

The Second Vatican Council concluded on 8 December 1965. It had begun on 11 October 1962, four months after Paddy's ordination. The Council's first document was *Sacrosanctum Concilium*, the Constitution on the Sacred Liturgy, promulgated on 4 December 1963. It called for the study of liturgy 'to be ranked among the compulsory and major courses in seminaries and religious houses of studies; in theological faculties it is to rank among the principal courses'. *Sacrosanctum Concilium* called for professors to be 'thoroughly trained for their work in institutes specialising in this subject'. The Irish Episcopal Conference appointed Paddy as the first Professor of Liturgy at Maynooth, effective 22 June 1965 but enabling him to take further studies at the Institut Supérieur de Liturgie in Paris. This graduate institute in liturgical studies had been established at the Institut Catholique de Paris in 1956. Its first director, Dom Bernard Botte OSB in his memoirs writes of having 'six or seven exceptionally qualified Irish students'. Paddy was one of them. He graduated as *Peritus in Sacra Liturgia* in 1968.

Paddy began lecturing in liturgy and sacramental theology at Maynooth in September 1968. Students recall lectures carefully prepared, delivered in a soft northern accent, beginning and ending on time, Paddy in the early days wearing the toga of the Sorbonne, walking from side to side on the rostrum in Loftus Hall. Examination questions called for an understanding of liturgy 'under its theological, historical, spiritual, pastoral and canonical aspects', as sought by *Sacrosanctum Concilium*. Paddy was strict and disciplined and it was a great surprise that he suffered serious illness in December 1980. Illness would mark his last years of earthly life.

As a member of the Faculty of Theology, Paddy played an active part, including as Dean of Theology, 1985–96. His work was marked by a great sense of workmanship, fairness and loyalty. As well as ensuring the place of liturgy within theological studies, he took full part in the deliberations of the Faculty in a time of renewal and, at times, of controversy. Over the years, Paddy became a senior and respected member of the Faculty. Colleagues saw a person of sharp mind and honest judgement and wit, with a reputation as a versifier.

His work was not confined to Loftus Hall. He served ten years as editor of the *Irish Theological Quarterly*. He was awarded an honorary doctorate by the Open University for his work on the theology programmes of Maryvale Institute in Birmingham, one of Maynooth's affiliated colleges, as they were called.

As a member of the National Liturgy Commission from its inception until 2013, and even before, he freely gave time and expertise to the Episcopal Conference in the renewal and reform of the liturgy. He also served for many years on the Advisory Committees on Church Music and Sacred Art and Architecture. To all this he brought a phenomenal memory. His historical and linguistic abilities were also available in his membership of the Advisory Committee of the International Commission on English in the Liturgy (ICEL), 1984–91. He was a member of its translation subcommittee until 1999 and continued to contribute to the work of translation as a member of what was known as 'the Irish group', with Fr Seán Collins OFM and Fr Tom Finan, 2005–7. In 2005 he was named a consultor of the Congregation for Divine Worship and Discipline of the Sacraments.

A close friend of the late Mgr Seán Swayne – another of the six or seven Paris students mentioned above – he helped to draw up the programme for the one-year course in liturgy at the Liturgy Centre founded at Mount St Anne's in 1974. Seán and Paddy were ably assisted in this task by Fr Liam G. Walsh OP and Fr J.D. Crichton, the doyen of liturgists in these islands. Paddy was a visiting lecturer at the Centre from its foundation and later when based in Carlow and, since 1996, at Maynooth College, and is remembered as a great friend and supporter of the Centre.

He retired as Professor of Liturgy at Maynooth after thirty years of service on 31 August 1998, becoming curate in the parish of Moville, Co. Donegal, Diocese of Derry. He was twenty-two years in Moville, the only parish in which he served, and parish life seemed to suit him from the start. He immediately immersed himself in pastoral work, especially in a ministry to the sick and dying. It could be a visit to a sick person at home or in hospital, or an almost daily visit to a dying parishioner. Though known as a man of academic ability, their priest, 'Father McGoldrick' was described as humble, gentle and holy. He formally retired as curate on 11 September 2020.

Paddy struggled with ill health during the past ten years, and especially as he moved to his family home in Buncrana in mid-March 2020. For Paddy, this was to be a short break but Covid-19 restrictions meant remaining there. He began writing. He had already one article written and it was given as a talk to fellow priests of Derry at a day of recollection in December 2019. From March to September 2020, he wrote seventeen more. The collection of articles, as he called them, are now this book, *Remember and Give Thanks*. They are reflections on the eucharist.

Paddy hoped that they might be published but never took any steps to do this nor gave instructions to do so. Editing has required putting the articles into a sequence other than the order of their writing. One article has become two chapters.

Apart from the first chapter, writing was done in a short period of time, just six months. Since Paddy's health declined so rapidly, he had no chance to revise or complete the last chapter, which he regarded as unfinished.

Chapters vary in length and are gathered into four sections. The first and last chapters were the first and last written. Sacred Scripture is cited throughout and references have been added. Let the reader also notice how often the eucharistic prayers are mentioned and quoted; these prayers tell our eucharistic faith.

Endnotes and an afterword have been added. The endnotes have given an opportunity to record some other writings over the years. The reader may read these reflections as spiritual moments on the gift of eucharist or as a course of study in understanding that gift. *Remember and Give Thanks.*

Acknowledgements

As a student of liturgy in the 1970s, I had met Paddy a few times and usually in the company of Seán Swayne. So much of our lives over the past forty years had connections with the National Centre for Liturgy. In our transfer from Carlow to Maynooth in 1996, Paddy was a true friend and supporter.

In the task of editing, I acknowledge the assistance of Moira Bergin, Julie Kavanagh, Liam Tracey and Tom Whelan. We have known Paddy in various ways and times: as students, as lecturers in liturgy, as associated with the National Commission for Liturgy, ICEL, the National Centre for Liturgy and Maynooth College.

The help and encouragement given by Paddy's sister and brothers, Caitríona, Brian and Neil, is gratefully acknowledged.

Aidan Chester, then director of Veritas, signalled his immediate readiness to publish. Colette Dower undertook the work of design and typesetting.

Patrick Jones, priest of Dublin diocese, was director of the National Centre for Liturgy, St Patrick's College, Maynooth and, as the Institute of Pastoral Liturgy, Carlow, 1992–2013.

Moira Bergin RSM, has been a staff member of the National Centre for Liturgy since 1993. She studied theology at Maynooth, 1988–91.

Julie Kavanagh also studied theology at Maynooth, 1986–9. She is a pastoral and liturgical resource person in the Diocese of Kildare and Leighlin.

Liam Tracey OSM, has taught liturgy at Maynooth since 1999, succeeding Patrick McGoldrick as Professor of Liturgy in 2002.

Tom Whelan CSSp, has lectured at Maynooth and has served with Patrick McGoldrick on ICEL and the national commission for liturgy.

eucharist ... in mystery

1
———————

Always and Everywhere to Give You Thanks[1]

In his autobiographical work *The Seven Storey Mountain*[2] Thomas Merton recounts an experience he had while in New York in late August and early September 1939. It was a time of great tension and foreboding, he recalls, even in that 'toughest of cities', as Europe moved ever closer to war. On his way to Mass on the first Friday of September he heard the news that German planes had bombed Warsaw. What struck him about the Mass (it was a High Mass) was that at the heart of it, even on that day, the priest still sang: *Vere dignum et iustum est, aequum et salutare, nos tibi semper et ubique gratias agere ...*

'Always and Everywhere to Give You Thanks.' Why is this so? Why is the central prayer of the central act of the Church always one of thanksgiving, even in such a dire situation, even in the circumstances in which I write this today, as the whole world struggles to deal with the inexorable spread of the coronavirus?

Eucharist
The basic answer is that at the Last Supper Jesus gave thanks over the bread and wine and that, ever since, this is what the Church has done in imitation of him and in obedience to his command: 'Do this in memory of me' (Lk 22:19; 1 Cor 11:24-25). In the course of the

Mass, as it has developed, the Church makes a solemn declaration of its thanksgiving to God in the eucharistic prayer. 'Eucharist' of course means thanksgiving, but from early times the word came to be used more widely also, both of the whole service with the eucharistic prayer at its core and of the bread and wine over which it was proclaimed. They had been 'eucharistised'. With its connotation of thanksgiving the word 'eucharist' took very firm root in Christian discourse, a word of great richness for us Christians, a word that, together with the action it denotes, joins in one communion all the generations of God's people right from the Lord himself.

But the Church gives thanks in the eucharist not just because that is what Christ did, as if its imitation of him might be largely of a formal or external kind or little more than an accident of history. From its imitation of the Lord and his words and actions, it has developed a deep conviction about and a profound insight into the centrality of thanksgiving in its worship and its life, a conviction and an insight that continue to inspire and sustain its practice. The Church gives thanks because it must, because it knows that it must.

The Eucharistic Prayer[3]

What form does this thanksgiving take? We have our answer in the eucharistic prayers themselves.

For most of its history the greater part of the Church in the West has used only the Roman Canon (Eucharistic Prayer I),[4] in which the theme of thanksgiving is stated emphatically in the Preface but with very little development there or later. Eastern Churches have had a much richer tradition, and it was the great eucharistic prayers of this tradition that provided the model for what is now our Eucharistic Prayer IV, composed in the early years after the Second Vatican Council.

'Thanksgiving' is not to be understood in an exclusive or narrow sense, because in these prayers we see that it flows over into and expresses itself in praise and blessing and glorification and acknowledgment and confession of God.

For what do we give thanks? Eucharistic Prayer IV begins with the mystery of God in himself: 'you are the one God living and true, existing before all ages and abiding for all eternity, dwelling in unapproachable light.' This calls to mind the words of the *Gloria*: 'We give you thanks for your great glory.' It is an acknowledgment simply of the transcendent reality of God in all its fullness, of the divine holiness and glory, and, faced with this mystery of God and what God is, we human beings can only express our admiration before God, our acknowledgment, and our gratitude that such indeed is our God. The prayer continues with its proclamation of God's creation and the great plan for all that God has made, a plan traced in the account of salvation history, the story of God's interaction with the people, right up to the incarnation of Christ in the fullness of time, then on to his life, death and resurrection and the sending of the Holy Spirit, and finally up to its climax in the Lord's second coming and the glorious fulfilment of all and of everything in Christ at the end of time.

This history is one both of human response to God's action and of repeated human failure too, but God never abandons his plan or people or creation; God remains present there, in all the world and in the ongoing life of humanity. It is an active presence of God, seeking to make known his great design and to advance it in spite of all human sin and of the continuing human failure to work towards its final fulfilment. God remains faithful to this purpose and will accomplish it even in and through and in spite of the ongoing history of human resistance and rejection.

Our Response of Thanksgiving

What God has done reveals something of what God is as God and of God's great project in creation; it reveals God's love for us, God's presence to us and his unceasing work on us and in us. We owe everything to God: we can claim no credit for any of it, not for creation, not for our own existence, not for our salvation at work all around us and in us, not for the hope it gives us. All is God's gift.[5]

Confronted with this realisation, we can only give thanks in response – thanksgiving expressing itself explicitly and in a whole range of forms and attitudes. Thanksgiving is not just a prayer or formulary of words. It invites us to a deeper level of understanding; it seeks to enter the heart and to become a disposition of soul and an attitude of life. It is for us to be in harmony with what it proclaims, to grow into it and to express it in ourselves and by our way of living, as people of grateful minds and hearts and souls and lives. Such thanksgiving brings us to God and it helps us to recognise more and more clearly the immense range and the profound depths of God's blessings and to return love for love in responding to them.

The Eucharist in the History of Salvation

At this point we should ask the question: is Eucharistic Prayer IV and the tradition on which it is modelled just an extended prayer developed to enhance the celebration of the eucharist, to highlight the sacredness and the solemnity of the occasion, or is it truly eucharistic in a deeper sense, in that what it expresses and develops and celebrates is the mystery at the very heart of the eucharist, arising out of that mystery and not just added from the outside to our liturgical celebration? To pose the question in a different way, do we learn something more about the eucharist itself from the great sweep of such prayers as Eucharistic Prayer IV?

Certainly we do. The history of salvation outlined there is not merely a sort of prelude but it enters into the eucharist as part of it. To put it the other way around, in celebrating the eucharist we are celebrating not only the Lord's actions at the Last Supper and the death and resurrection which followed. This is indeed the core of the eucharist, but in Christ's paschal mystery, anticipated by him sacramentally in what he did at the Last Supper, his whole life is summed up and completed. All his mission, all the direction of his life, all that motivated and inspired him right through from the beginning, all of that has brought him to this moment and is somehow present there in him now, in his body on the cross and in his actions at the Last Supper, in which he anticipated this in mystery.

But Christ has a still wider role in the divine plan. The whole history of salvation was directed to him. From the beginning God was making ready for the incarnation, working on the conditions that would lead to it. In God's own time and way, the Jewish people are prepared to produce in Mary one who could be the mother of his Son. It was a long and tortuous history, with many failures through human sin and many setbacks. But God persevered throughout and in the fullness of time all was ready for the coming of God's Son among us in our nature. In God's design and by God's grace all this immense labour came to its fulfilment in Christ, and in that sense continues to be present in him. In himself Christ sums up and embodies all that God has worked to accomplish.

This means that in the eucharist, as Christ gives it to us, the whole project of God, the whole history of creation and of salvation as proclaimed in Eucharistic Prayer IV, is somehow present. And not just present – active too. Because that project of God will not reach its full accomplishment until Christ's second coming. In the meantime, God's work in the world and in the people goes on, as it did all through the Old Testament and before it, and the eucharist celebrates this and looks forward to it; it confirms our place in it; it commits us to it and itself advances it. The heart of the eucharist is not a timeless, unchanging, other-worldly mystery but one that sweeps us up in its forward dynamic march towards the consummation which God is ceaselessly at work to achieve.

What Eucharistic Prayer IV presents to us so fully as reason for our thanksgiving, all of that we enter into every time we come together for the eucharist; as the Church and as individual Christians we are caught up in it, with all that it demands of us in our prayer, our motivation, our daily living.

Can we take a step further? By Christ's gift, the bread and wine, sanctified by the Lord's own words and by the Holy Spirit, become his body and blood. Here the dynamic driving the eucharistic prayer forward reaches a new and higher level: in these eucharistic gifts, held up for our veneration and offered to us for our consumption, there is manifested a sacramental expression and recapitulation of the divine-human interplay of salvation up to and including its first climax in the event of Christ. This dynamic will continue to drive the prayer forward, because, under these signs of his sacrificial death, it is the Lord as he is now who is present, the Lord in the fullness of his resurrection and ascension. In him God's great plan is completed already – but not yet in us, his brothers and sisters, not yet in all of creation. And so in the eucharistic body and blood present before us there is also a sacramental anticipation of the long course of this salvation history that still remains to be lived, and of its final consummation in Christ when he comes again in his glory. May we say that the eucharistic gifts themselves embody all that the prayer, with its magnificent breadth and sweep, proclaims and celebrates?

Thanksgiving, Offering, Petition

For the most part, it is true, it is only in the first half of the prayer that this theme of thanksgiving is explicit. But indeed the prayer is eucharistic throughout, up to the final Great Amen. In the second part of the prayer our thanksgiving expresses itself in offering and petition.

The momentum of the prayer carries us beyond words of thanksgiving into the very presence of that for which we give thanks, but thanksgiving is still the frame of mind and spirit in which we seek to enter these deeper riches of this mystery. And if we recall the universal extent of the effects of the mystery, right to the limits of creation and to the whole of humanity and to the end of time, then it is right that our thanksgiving for God's gift should also take the form of petition, petition that these effects be realised everywhere in Church and world through the transforming and renewing and perfecting power of the Holy Spirit, petition that they be realised in the world to come among the faithful departed and all who have died in God's mercy, petition that all of us be united one day with Christ and with one another in God's new creation.

And indeed, however skilfully and beautifully our expression of thanksgiving may be composed, however deep the faith with which we proclaim it, however fully we may be living it in our hearts and in our lives, this expression of our thanksgiving is not our final word. Eucharistic Prayer III, remembering Christ's death and resurrection, and looking forward to his second coming, says: 'we offer you in thanksgiving this holy and living sacrifice.' The memorial that the Church makes is of such depth and power as to give rise to an offering, and the offering that we make is not our own in its core but Christ's. Even our thanksgiving in its highest expression is itself given to us as a gift by God, and so it surpasses all that we of ourselves could ever say or do. It calls to mind the words of Common Preface IV: 'although you have no need of our praise, yet our thanksgiving is itself your gift, since our praises add nothing to your greatness but profit us for salvation, through Christ our Lord.'

Thanksgiving in the Face of Evil and Suffering

To return to Thomas Merton at Mass that day in New York. 'Always and Everywhere to Give You Thanks' – must we then give thanks to God for all the evil in the world, all the injustice and exploitation and violence and abuse, all the illness, the coronavirus, and natural disasters of every kind? When I was a young altar boy, the parish priest used to quote from time to time in his sermons a simple poem. It thanked God for all God's blessings, for this and for that, and the last line was: 'Thanks be to God that what is, is so.' Can we agree with this? If it is our duty as Christians to seek to overcome evils of every kind in the world, if this is part of the work God expects of us for the fulfilment of God's plan, what truth can there be, if any, in the last line of this poem?

Confronted with the supreme reality of God and the mystery of God, human affairs and human understanding must take their proper, subordinate, place. We believe that God is present in all our human situations, even in ills of all kinds. And when the happenings of life or our own actions place us there, that is where we must seek

God, actively seek God, and that is where we shall find him. Evil and catastrophe are part of the world created good by God. From the beginning God allowed for this, and, if God permits it, then God must have a purpose even there. If this is so, it must have a role to play in the outworking of his design, a design that is always one of love. God is there, even in the midst of such evil, and God can use this too in the fulfilment of his will, working on us his people to prepare us for the good that he has always intended for us. The history of the Old Testament makes this very clear, and history is still on its way to the goal God has for it. Nothing is wasted by God or beyond God's transforming power. In God's skilled hands, even such things become means by which he will achieve his purpose: the new creation, the new heavens and the new earth, the new humanity, the new you and I.

With an understanding such as this, the Church can thank God that what is, is so, while all the time striving to change what is but should not be so or, if this is not possible, engaging with the situation as it is in whatever ways it can. It can thank God for what God is in himself, for God's active presence with us and God's love and higher purpose, right there touching us, even in circumstances of disaster and evil, working to turn these to our good.

Suffering is an iron law of life. It was so in Jesus' life and he confirmed this for his disciples by his words and his example. We give thanks *in* suffering but do we give thanks *for* suffering? What disciple, present that afternoon on the hill of Calvary, could have found anything for which to give thanks to God? And yet, ever since, what took place there has been at the heart of the Church's thanksgiving. We do give thanks to God for what Christ suffered or at least we come very close to it. We give thanks for all that his passion and death achieved for us, but this is not for the suffering considered in itself. It is for the presence of the Father to Christ, despite appearances, in and all through it; it is for that suffering as accepted willingly by Christ out of his obedience to the Father and out of his love for all the world. It is for that suffering thus transformed, given its redemptive power and made life-giving, by the faithfulness with which he embraced it and lived it right to the end.

St Paul has his own specifically Christian insight of faith to share with us. He speaks of his completing in his own flesh what is lacking in the afflictions of Christ for the sake of his body, the Church (Col 1:24-25). That is the privileged role that God in his wisdom and love has assigned to us in the realisation of his plan – and not just for the good of the Church but for the well-being and the salvation of the whole world.

In the circumstances of the coronavirus as it spreads, we are being reminded frequently that we are all in this together. This is a truth of much wider application, because even as individuals we are always part of the wider communion that makes us one. Suffering willingly borne is part of the contribution that God invites from all of us and each of us. It will bring its pain and its sorrow, but true understanding together with firm faith, hope and trust can find comfort there and can draw a response even of thanksgiving. By his endurance of his own suffering Christ has made this possible for us and he has given the example for us to follow.

I was struck by the account of the martyrdom of St Paul Miki and his companions in the Office of Readings on 6 February. Facing their imminent death by crucifixion and the spear, three of them are explicitly recorded as giving thanks to God, thanks that clearly came from the heart.

'Always and Everywhere to Give You Thanks.' No doubt from another starting point and using different words and categories of thought one could also present this mystery in all its fullness. But the Church has not been mistaken in placing thanksgiving at the heart of its prayer and so of its life, and in continuing to insist on it.

We started with the experience of Thomas Merton in a church in New York on a day of anxiety and fear. But from there our theme of thanksgiving has brought us into the immensity of God, God's holiness and glory, into the richness of God's inner life, into the love, the abundance, the generosity, the wisdom of God's plan; it has brought us into the great whole of which we, all together and each individually, are part; it has brought us into the process of growth and transformation that God is always overseeing and directing and correcting and moving forward on its course to the great fulfilment. By God's grace and power all of that is somehow made present in the eucharist and draws us into it. In what better way could we begin to respond than by giving thanks?

The Eucharist: A Sacrament of All Creation?

Among the great truths that the spread of the coronavirus and the attempts to counteract it have been making very clear to us is the interconnectedness of the whole world, of things and people, and more particularly the interdependence and the unity of the human race.

Sacrament

'Sacrament' is a word with a long and rich history in Christian tradition. Of itself 'sacrament' suggests a connection to the sacred, and through the centuries this has indeed been there. In the early Latin version of St Paul's letters it served to translate the Greek word *musterion*, which meant the hidden plan of God revealed in Christ. At least in a general way it retained something of this ever afterwards.

For St Augustine,[6] for example, it was a sacred sign.[7] There were many sacraments, signs that pointed beyond themselves to something sacred. But a sacrament was more than a finger indicating a distant, otherwise absent reality. Rather, in some sense the sacrament was itself filled with this reality and revealed it, served to make it present and active in the here and now.

In mediaeval times 'sacrament' came to be greatly reduced in its reference and was used exclusively of what, ever since, we call 'the seven sacraments'. These were defined much more narrowly as visible signs of invisible grace instituted by our Lord Jesus Christ.

While this brought the benefit of greater clarity regarding the seven, it also brought a notable weakening of the wider, more all-embracing understanding that gave these seven sacraments the context out of which in a sense they had emerged for special consideration. We have been the poorer for the loss. 'Sacramental', used as a noun, is a weaker word.

In this chapter 'sacrament' frequently reverts to its older, more comprehensive meaning. Rather than seeing the seven sacraments just in isolation, it is helpful to view them as the high points of a more extensive and varied landscape. This does not call into question at all anything that the Church teaches about the seven sacraments. It is concerned rather with the wider setting in which earlier centuries had placed them and had considered them.

A Sacramental World

We live in a sacramental world. For believers, all creation comes from God and of itself is good. Whatever science may establish, whatever theories there may be about its origin, creation will continue to speak to us of God, the God whose handiwork ultimately it is. In revealing something of its divine maker to us, it brings him somehow closer to us and to our lives; we believe that we find God in his works, an encounter that has been initiated by God and seeks a response from us.

That world enters into us. In God's design, it is from the earth that the human race took its origin at some time and in some way in the past, and the earth continues to sustain us in a great variety of indispensable ways. The world is always part of us as we are of it. Because of this, and coming as it does from God, it is a sacred place for us, a sacred environment for the life and the development of the human family.

This is an understanding that Jesus too shared, as we can see from the way he spoke of the world around him and from the way that he related to it and used it. He drew many images from that world and from the daily interaction of human beings with it as illustrations and expressions of his message. We may think of his parables, the process of sowing the seed, its growth, the harvest, for example, or the life and work of the shepherd, or his own experience of fishing. Clearly, the world around him had entered deeply into his mind. It had helped to shape his thought and his understanding, and so images from it came readily to him as instruments of his teaching.

But it went beyond teaching. Jesus used things of the earth as means of healing and of providing for people in their need. Thus, he cured many by his touch but he also used spittle and dust to make a paste, which he applied to the eyes of a blind man, before sending him to wash in the pool of Siloam. He turned water into a great quantity of wine at the wedding feast in Cana, the first of his signs, St John says (Jn 2:11), and by it he manifested his glory. He used loaves and fish to feed the hungry crowd in the wilderness and he then went on to use this to speak of his gift of the eucharist, his feeding of his people on his own body and blood.

The world around him entered even into his inner life, into his relationship with his Father. Thus, he went into the desert to pray and to fast; he went up into the hills or sought out a quiet place to be alone in his communion with the Father. He went to the river Jordan to be baptised by John, and there had the experience of being addressed by the Father as the beloved Son in whom he was well pleased, followed by the descent of the Holy Spirit upon him in the form of a dove.

In the embodiment of incarnation Jesus, Son of God, brought God into our world and into our human experience in a new way. By living his inner life and his relationship with the Father here on earth in a human body and as one of us, he made God known to those he encountered – not just in words but through being the sort of man he showed himself to be and through the life he lived and over the whole range of his human activity. These are the ways that are most familiar to us, the ways in which we reveal ourselves to one another.

For Jesus this is indeed a sacramental world; it is the general background to be kept in mind as we reflect on his words and actions at the Last Supper, where he took bread and wine and used them to give himself in his own body and blood to be food and drink for the sustenance of his people.

Bread and Wine

Bread and wine are more than a product of individuals for individuals. There is an important social component in both their making and their use, and so in their significance for us. We can think of the process by which the seed is sown, harvested, milled, made available and baked. We can go on to think of the family gathering at the table every day for their meals (though in the present, sad to say, this is becoming less and less a feature of our fragmented and individualist culture). We can think of the wider gatherings of friends and neighbours for special occasions, where the heart of the event is the meal taken together; we can think of the communal effect of this on the whole group and on its individual members. The food and drink shared are signs of what it is that gathers the group together and gives it a certain unity, and at the same time they are means of renewing and strengthening it.

The Bread and Wine of the Eucharist

One of the most enriching changes made in the *Roman Missal* after the Second Vatican Council was the replacement of the old prayers of the Offertory by the new compositions – new in their content, wording and arrangement, but not in their genre or form. They are modelled on the ancient Jewish tradition of *berakah* or prayer of blessing, a blessing of God made in this case over bread and wine.

There are several rich seams to be mined in these two prayers. It is as if the Church, taking the bread and wine that it will use in the eucharist, pauses for a moment to reflect: Where have these come from? Why are we about to use them? What are they to become?

Ultimately they are from God the Creator, from the bountiful goodness of God's creation, as fruits of the earth and of what it yields. In themselves then they are divine gifts that we can only receive, and so we begin by acknowledging this in a prayer of blessing of God.

But if they are gifts that the Church, along with all humanity, has first received, they are gifts that we must work on in order to make them our own, to adapt them to the use that God intends us to make of them as food and drink for our life's journey. That empowering of us, of course, is itself another gift from God. And so the prayer of blessing recognises in them both fruit of the earth or of the vine, and work of human hands. It is with this understanding of faith that we take the bread and wine of the eucharist and offer them to God.

What does it mean to 'offer' here? It is a solemn act of recognition before God of this fuller reality, of the truth of what they are. God, of course, does not need to have this offering made to him, it is we who need to make it. These are not just elements of food and drink that we may take for granted but gifts of God first and fruits of divine-human collaboration, as are so many of the things that we have and use in our daily lives. As part of our preparation of bread and wine for use in the eucharist we give them back symbolically as a sort of first fruits to God, from whom ultimately they have come. This is not the great offering of the Mass, nor even an anticipation of it, though obviously it cannot be separated from it either and will be caught up into it when it is made later in the eucharistic prayer.

Now that we have acknowledged where the bread and wine have come from and what they represent, the two prayers look to the reason they have been brought to the eucharist and what they are to become. The gift of the earth made into the human reality of bread will become the bread of life for us; the fruit of the vine made into the human reality of wine will become our spiritual drink. All of this gives us good reason for blessing God, whose work it is in the first place and by whose gracious gift the Church and we its members have part in this eucharist here and now.

In the eucharist these natural realities of bread and wine and human meals will find an unexpected fulfilment, but at a level far beyond their natural purpose or power. On the eve of his passion, Jesus gathered around him his closest associates, his apostles, his friends, as he called them, for a last meal together before his death, a meal that they would always remember and would understand better as they looked back on it in the light of his passion and resurrection. 'Do this in memory of me,' he said (Lk 22:19; 1 Cor 11:24-25). In our use of bread and wine in obedience to his command, all creation together with all that is good in human activity will be taken up into the greater mystery of the eucharist, when God's transforming power makes of them Christ's body and blood for our journey to the world to come. Caught up into this mystery in a similar way will be our human meals at their best, with all that they express and all that they strive after. By Christ's grace the natural food and drink we take for our sustenance are there transformed into food and drink that will give and will sustain a higher life. So too the intimacy of the family meal and the fellowship of our celebratory meals in all their richness will be transcended in the eucharist and there become a communion with Christ and with one another in Christ that far surpasses this human dimension. 'Because the bread is one,' St Paul says, 'we, though many, are one body, because we all eat of the one bread' (1 Cor 10:17). Our unity in this communion is its fruit.

Bread Given for the Life of the World
Bread given: given to whom? Jesus' actual words can be translated in two different though closely related ways. 'The bread that I shall give is my flesh for the life of the world' or 'The bread that I shall give for the life of the world is my flesh' (Jn 6:51). Is it the bread as given by Jesus to his disciples, his body given to them for their life? This is the first and more obvious interpretation. But there is another possible reading of what Christ meant. The bread is that body given up to his Father in his passion and death, and at the Last Supper given sacramentally in anticipation of this, given in what he said and did

there and in the bread and wine he used. That bread and wine become the very life of the world, as he promised, and the life of the disciples who will receive it from him. This is closer to Jesus' words over the bread at the Last Supper: 'This is my body, which will be given up for you' (Lk 22:19) – given up willingly to death and in that act given up to the Father in obedience, faithfulness and love as a redemptive sacrifice for the world. It is this body thus given that Jesus offers to his disciples then and ever since to take and eat, enabling them to participate in all the saving power of his sacrifice as they receive from him and from the Father the food of life.

We do not have to decide between the two interpretations. In the rich depths of Jesus' words and actions, and in the mystery of the eucharist as it comes to us from him, both are true.

God's One Creation

In the Old Testament, particularly in many of the psalms and in the great canticle of Daniel 3, those praying call on all creation to join with them in the praise of God. It is as if they felt some close bond that united themselves and the world around them before God, as if that human prayer somehow gives voice to the inarticulate praise that creation by its very existence is always giving to its Creator.

Similarly, Eucharistic Prayer IV in its introduction to the *Sanctus* says: 'With them [the countless hosts of angels] we, too, confess your name in exultation, giving voice to every creature under heaven, as we acclaim ...' The *Sanctus* is presented here as the praise of all the created things of the universe, given voice in our prayer, all as one caught up into the great hymn of the whole court of heaven – God's entire creation united in acclamation of its all-holy Creator. It is a very powerful expression of the unity before God that holds together all that exists.

What about the world to come? Is this unity to be broken at the end of time? Will the world of nature continue to exist then or will it disappear completely? We can say at least that it will survive in us, the human race, transformed in heaven, in that all through our lives on earth it entered into us, it helped to make us what we are in life and at death. And so, when God's people and individual human beings pass over into glory, the world of nature is transformed and made new in them. At the end, the earth, the world, the universe will have fulfilled what God had created them to be and to do, and, even if they cease to be then, something of them will still endure in what is the high point of God's creation, as we know it, its greatest achievement. They will have their place in the new human race and the new human being.

We can see this in a fundamental doctrine of our faith. From the beginning the Church has had a profound conviction that Christ's resurrection embraced his full bodily reality. The transformation wrought in him in his glorification is a transformation of body as well as of soul and spirit. The incarnation did not come to an end in his death but endures for all eternity in him in heaven.

In Christ's resurrection God gives us the promise of our resurrection too, in all our bodiliness. St Paul insists on this at some length (1 Cor 15:12-58), and we profess our faith in it every time that we say in the Creed: 'the resurrection of the body' (or of the flesh). In Christ's entry into glory, and ours, something of God's creation in all its materiality enters too.

But can we go further? Scripture speaks of the new heavens and the new earth, and the concluding part of Eucharistic Prayer IV seems to envisage a fuller form of existence for the universe. It presents a magnificent vision of the kingdom of God in all its perfection: 'There [in your kingdom], with the whole of creation, freed from the corruption of sin and death, may we glorify you through Christ our Lord ...' It is important to note the ambiguity of this translation. Who or what is to be freed from corruption? It could be read to mean that the prayer is speaking here about us, but in fact it is clear from the Latin original that it is about all creation, with ourselves included of course. Somehow all creation is to be there, transformed, made new, and we as an integral part of it, all united in the glorification of God.

In Romans 8 St Paul links together very closely the human race and all creation both in this world and in their future state (Rm 8:18-39). Creation is waiting with eager longing for the revealing of God's children, he says. It is only then, he implies, that it will become what God intended it to be from the beginning. And later on he adds that creation itself will be set free from its bondage to decay and obtain the glorious liberty of God's children. This consummation, he seems to suggest, is something for which the whole of creation itself was made, and until it is attained all of creation will continue to groan in travail, seeking to bring it forth, as it were. Similarly, we ourselves continue to groan inwardly too as we wait for the full status of our adoption as God's children to be attained and revealed in us, and this involves our redemption in all our bodily reality.

Here in this world and in death too, the state of all creation and the state of God's children are intimately intertwined. By God's design they belong together and this unity in the totality of creation will endure. God himself will perfect it in the new heavens, the new earth, the new humanity – the new creation – of the world to come.

To say this is not to imply that all people, whatever sort of lives they lived, whatever their standing before God at death, will be saved. God alone will be the judge of that.

The Bread of Heaven, The Wine of the Kingdom

This consideration of the broader background has not been a distraction from our main theme, because it contributes to a wider understanding of the eucharist.

Up to this point, in trying to grasp a little more of the breadth of the eucharistic mystery we have been looking predominantly at both the past and the present. Now it is time to see what we may learn from it about the future.

As we have seen earlier, the wider world of creation and of human work, present in the bread and wine of the eucharist, is sanctified and transcended by God's creative act in transforming that bread and wine into the body and blood of Christ and giving it to be consumed by us. But this in its turn gives us a sign of the new world of heaven and earth.

Christian tradition has always acknowledged in our reception of Christ's body and blood a salvific effect in body as well as in soul. This is not to be reduced to good health. As we consume the bread of life, our bodies together with our souls are being drawn more deeply into God's great purpose: they are being made ready for the resurrection of both as the single entity that we are.

Thus, the eucharist confirms God's promise to us and to his wider creation and indeed anticipates it in sacrament. The new world is already coming into being there. Even now, by Christ's grace and power, elements of creation are instrumental in preparing the new creation that is God's plan.

This future is already realised in Christ in glory, and he becomes for us both our food and drink for the journey there, and the food and drink of the divine feast of heaven when the journey is completed. As given by Christ at the Last Supper, his body and blood come to us under the sign of his sacrificial death, but now it is Christ, risen and ascended, who is present to us there in all his glory. In the eucharist then, bread and wine of the earth, transformed by God's creative act and to be consumed by us as Christ's body and blood, are caught up into the glory of Christ in heaven, and so for us and for all creation they are even now a sacramental but utterly real anticipation of what they promise: the new creation that is God's project finally completed in all its fullness. All will return to the original unity from which it started, a unity that in God's eyes it never lost, despite the complexity of its development and despite the disintegrating effect of human mismanagement and misuse and the corrupting effect of human sin – a state of integration and unity before God at the end that will far surpass all that it could ever have known or imagined.

By the Working of the Holy Spirit

A brief consideration of the role of the Holy Spirit will confirm this. God's Spirit has been at work on and in the world from the very act of creation. Throughout the erratic course of Jewish history, it was the Spirit who was guiding events and hearts and lives in order to prepare a people and a woman ready and worthy both to produce and to receive God's incarnate Son. The Spirit was actively present in Jesus' life, from his conception, through his early life and his public ministry and then in the culmination towards which that life had been leading, his death and his resurrection. This is the Spirit, sent in a new way by the risen Christ from the Father, who will be present and active in the Church and world until the great divine plan is fully realised.

It is the role of the Holy Spirit then, from the beginning, to work all through history to advance God's project and to bring it to the final accomplishment that is God's will.

Eucharistic Prayer IV, at the end of its long account of salvation history, says that the risen Christ sent the Holy Spirit from the Father 'so that, bringing to perfection his work in the world, he might sanctify creation to the full'. 'Perfect' and 'sanctify' are traditional words often used of the Holy Spirit in such a context; the work done by Christ during his life on earth is to be continued in the world and brought to its complete fulfilment by the Spirit.

To turn to the role of the Holy Spirit in the eucharist. This is not a different or unrelated work. It is the same Spirit carrying out the same mission, but now in the eucharist. Eucharistic Prayer IV moves on immediately to make this clear: 'May this same Holy Spirit graciously sanctify these offerings ...' There is a similar connection of thought in Eucharistic Prayer III. The effect of the Spirit's coming upon the bread and wine and sanctifying them is that they become Christ's body and blood. In continuity with this, later on the prayer will ask that we who receive this one bread and one chalice may ourselves become by the Spirit's power one body, one spirit in Christ. The other eucharistic prayers introduced into the *Roman Missal* after the Second Vatican Council make a similar petition and in similar language. As it is the Spirit whose sanctifying power transforms our bread and wine into Christ's eucharistic body, so it is the Spirit too who will transform us who receive that body into Christ's ecclesial body. What the Spirit does in every eucharist is what the Spirit is always engaged in down through the ages and all over the world.

This is a unity that has still to be worked towards in our lives and in the world, and it will never be reached fully here on earth. We bring those lives to the eucharist and we bring the eucharist back to those lives. The Holy Spirit is at work in both to achieve the final unity of all in God's kingdom.

What holds all of this together is the one great purpose of God, which is being worked out from the first particle of matter and will continue until all is brought to its completion, when, in the fullness of time, all is finally gathered into one by God in Christ. In Christ: because, as St Paul tells us: 'He is the image of the invisible God, the first-born of all creation; for in him all things were created, in heaven and on earth, visible and invisible … all things were created through him and for him. He is before all things, and in him all things hold together. He is the head of the body, the Church; he is the beginning, the first-born from the dead, that in everything he might be pre-eminent. For in him all the fullness of God was pleased to dwell, and through him to reconcile to himself all things, whether on earth or in heaven, making peace by the blood of his cross' (Col 1:15-20).

Our community, our congregation, any one of us may be just a dot in the great universe and its history, but, small though we may be, by God's gracious gift we are unique parts of it with our unique roles to play.

Over the centuries the eucharist has been given many titles. With an understanding such as this, may we speak of it too as a sacrament of all creation: a sacrament of our world as it is in God's plan, a sacrament of our world as it will be when God brings his plan to its glorious fulfilment?

God's ways are not our ways. In recent times a lot has been spoken and written about the interconnectedness and interdependence of everything in the universe and about the unity of the human race. But, in God's wisdom, has it taken the spread of the tiny coronavirus to bring sharply home to us something of what these abstract words may actually mean in real terms? And for us Christians has it a lesson even in theology?

Christ, Church, Sacrifice

For some decades now we have not been speaking about sacrifice in the way we once did. 'Sacrifice,' with its associated terms 'offering', 'oblation', 'victim', 'altar', 'host', 'priest', is one of the great words of our Christian tradition, as it is of religions generally. We used to speak a lot of the sacrifice of Christ and of the sacrifice of the Mass; we spoke of the offering of oneself or of smaller acts of self-denial as sacrifices. But for the past five or six decades the word has been dropping quietly out of our vocabulary.

Part of the reason for this, no doubt, has been the rediscovery or the retrieval of other words from our tradition, with the broadening and the enriching of our eucharistic vocabulary, and the growth in understanding that this has been bringing. Even the word 'eucharist' itself: I got a letter from an elderly bishop in the late 1960s seeking my opinion on the rapidly increasing frequency in our use of the word 'eucharist' in the Catholic Church then, and asking if it was not rather a Protestant name. I understood what he meant in raising the matter and why he asked the question. We knew the word at the time, of course, but it did not have the familiar and regular place that it has acquired since in our ordinary religious vocabulary. And even as recently as that, to Catholic ears it still had something of a Protestant ring.

The Second Vatican Council and what flowed from it have had effects of the greatest importance on our understanding, our practices, our vocabulary, our celebration of the eucharist. We do not see the eucharist or speak of it or experience it in just the same way as we did, say, sixty or seventy years ago. This is part of a normal pattern that goes with the passage of time.

But as overall it has been to our great gain to rediscover and to reintroduce words and practices and understandings of the eucharist that had slipped into the background, so it would be a great loss to allow this to happen now to our vocabulary of sacrifice, and with it to the rich history and the rich understanding that the word opens up to us.

The Sacrifice of the Eucharist

Why do we speak of the eucharist as a sacrifice? Why has this term been part of our eucharistic vocabulary from the time of the early Church?

As a result of the controversies that arose at the time of the Reformation, Catholic theologians made several attempts in the centuries that followed to formulate a definition of sacrifice as understood and practised in religions generally and in the Old Testament in particular, and then to show that such definitions were realised in the case of the Catholic eucharist. These attempts tended to be contrived and unconvincing. But this effort raised a more basic question: should we be starting at all from some human definition or construct, to which the eucharist must then be seen to conform? Is it not rather the event of Christ, and his passion and death in particular, that should be our point of reference from the outset?

The eucharist is called a sacrifice surely because in the first place it is the sacrament of Christ's sacrifice. If 'sacrifice' is an appropriate term to use of Christ's passion and death, then it is an appropriate term for the ritual that he left us as the great memorial of his sacrifice. In the eucharist we imitate what Christ said and did at the Last Supper. This is a command that he laid on us, and, in obeying it, we are enabled by his gift to be joined to him, to relive with him here and now in ourselves and in our lives the mystery of his cross, to be drawn by him into all its meaning and its saving power.

The eucharist is the sacrament of Christ's sacrifice. But this pushes our question further back: why do we speak of Christ's passion and death as a sacrifice?

The Sacrifice of Christ

Again, it is important to get our starting point right. We use human language and institutions to speak of the event of Christ, but in doing so we must always remember that Christ goes beyond all our attempts to categorise or to portray him; he transcends all our religious institutions however venerable and well-established they may be, however sacred even. It is he who sets the standards for them rather than they for him. But we have no other language or set of references, and so we still need these to help us to understand Christ and what he did.

At the Last Supper Jesus anticipated his passion and death: his words and actions there have a sacrificial reference and tone and draw us into the sacrificial understanding that he had of what he was about to do. And indeed the timing of the Last Supper and of Christ's death, call immediately to mind the Jewish Passover, the sacrifice of the paschal lamb and the special meal that followed. Already at a very early stage St Paul uses the Passover to speak of Christ's death: 'Christ, our paschal lamb, has been sacrificed' (1 Cor 5:7). The gospel of St John places that death at just the time the paschal lambs were being sacrificed in the Temple. And in referring to the body of Christ immediately after his death, when the soldiers came to break his legs, he quotes from prescriptions about the paschal lamb: 'These things took place that the scriptures might be fulfilled: "Not a bone of him shall be broken"' (Jn 19:36; Ex 12:46; Ps 34 (33):21).

Such a sacrificial interpretation of Christ's great act on the cross had been prepared for by a growing spiritualising of the understanding of sacrifice in the Old Testament. In the psalms and the prophets there had developed an awareness that cultic sacrifice of itself is insufficient, indeed it can be empty. It must express an inner disposition, a proper attitude of mind and soul, a genuine turning of the offerers in themselves to God. One quotation from Psalm 51 (50), the great psalm of repentance, can stand for many: 'My sacrifice a contrite spirit, a humbled, contrite heart you will not spurn' (19). Where this is absent, the ritual sacrifice is null and void, unacceptable to God.

Similarly in the case of the ritual sacrifice of one whose conduct does not conform to the true meaning of sacrifice. Thus, for example, through the prophet Isaiah God castigates those who present the ritual offering while guilty of oppressing others, acting unjustly, neglecting the needs of the weak and the poor. The sacrifice pleasing to God is that made from a pure heart and a blameless life (Is 1:11-17, 58:1-14).

Life's Journey to Calvary

In the incarnation the Son of God takes on our nature. This means that the life he lives over the whole range of its activities is the living out in human terms of his relationship as Son to the Father. This relationship within the Trinity will express itself now in alignment of his will with the Father's, in total obedience and in unity of purpose. This is not to suggest that all of this was fully clear to Jesus at all times and from the beginning or that it was easy for him to do. He had to mature as a human being, with the struggle of mind to discern that purpose and the struggle of will to carry it out. But what characterised his life on earth was his whole-hearted intent on learning the divine will and obeying it faithfully.

This is why the author of Hebrews can put on Jesus' lips as he came into the world the words of Psalm 40 (39): 'Here I am, O God, I come to do your will' (Heb 10:7, 9; Ps 40 (39):6-9). Jesus emphasises this himself several times during the course of his public ministry, especially in the gospel of John (for example, Jn 4:34, 5:30, 6:38); he confirms it in his agony in the garden in the prayer he makes to the Father (Mt 26:39, 42; Lk 22:42; Mk 14:36); and until his death on Calvary he remains faithful.

This is the sacrifice that the author of Hebrews recognises (Heb 10:5-10). Psalm 40 (39) is quoted at some length: what God wants is an open ear rather than the multiplicity of ritual holocausts and offerings. 'Here I am, I come to do your will' (6-9), as we have seen, are words from the psalm that the author uses to sum up Jesus' whole intent.

It is important in our thinking about Christ's sacrifice not to separate his life and his death. He did not die as the result of some infection he caught as he travelled in Galilee or of an unfortunate accident that befell him in Jerusalem. He died because of his whole-hearted commitment to the mission he had been given by the Father. It was the intensity and the fullness of this commitment that brought him directly to Calvary and the cross. His death then recapitulates the motivation and the direction of his entire life. But it is not just another act of obedience on his part, like so many others before. It is the final, definitive, irrevocable act that sets the seal on a whole life. In trying to understand what his sacrifice is we must take all of this into account.

This is the offering that will please God. This single sacrifice made once for all by Jesus is of a quite different order from the multiple, endlessly repeated offerings of the Old Testament. Christ's sacrifice surpasses all of these, and in doing so it transcends all that they tried to express and to achieve but of themselves could never accomplish.

There is one particular text, from the prophet Malachi, that can serve as a transition from the sacrifices of the Old Testament to the new dispensation inaugurated by Christ. It had a strong influence in the early Church and on the eucharist, an influence that lasts to the present: 'I have no pleasure in you, says the Lord of hosts, and I will not accept an offering from your hand. For from the rising of the sun to its setting, my name is great among the nations and in every place incense is offered to my name, and a pure offering; for my name is great among the nations, says the Lord of hosts' (Mal 1:10-11). The early Church recognised that this text was fulfilled and surpassed in its eucharist.

At the beginning Christians were very cautious in their use of Jewish cultic terms about their own cultic practices. Later, however, when Christians and Jews had separated, when the temple had been destroyed by the Romans, when the true nature of Christ's priesthood and his sacrifice had embedded itself in Christian understanding, the Church began to use the language of sacrifice and of priesthood in a cultic context, but now it is always to be understood in the light of what Christ was in himself and what he had accomplished in his death.

That use has continued through the centuries. It caused controversy and division at the time of the Reformation, and something of that still endures, but the Catholic Church has found that the use of 'sacrifice' and 'priesthood' and related words is enlightening and enriching in its understanding and its celebration of the eucharist.

Our present *Roman Missal*, formed and revised and consolidated over many centuries, bears witness to this in the extent of words and images related to sacrifice that it contains. The most venerable of all is the Roman Canon (Eucharistic Prayer I), which contains a lot of cultic sacrificial words, particularly in its first part. This was the one eucharistic prayer in exclusive use in most of the Church of the West from ancient times until new eucharistic prayers were added after the Second Vatican Council. Such a history of use as the central prayer of the central act of the Church for such a long time and over such a wide area gives it a place apart in the history of Christian worship, for the influence it has had over many centuries, for the tradition of understanding that it has passed on and that has continued to enrich it, for the weight of prayer and of faith that it has carried.

Spiritual Sacrifice?
The term 'spiritual sacrifice' is already present in 1 Peter (1 Pt 2:5) and has continued in use ever since. But it can be understood in a

rather superficial way. If we apply it to the great offering made by Christ, we must be careful to recognise its true depth. In no sense does 'spiritual' suggest anything secondary here, as if it were only a substitute for the true sacrifice. The author of Hebrews says that Christ offered himself to God through the eternal Spirit (Heb 9:14). God's Spirit was present in Jesus throughout the whole of his life, guiding and directing it, bringing that life to its culmination in the cross of Calvary. In that sense we may speak of his offering as a spiritual sacrifice, a sacrifice made in the Holy Spirit.

We can recognise another dimension too. One of Jesus' last words on the cross was, 'Father, into your hands I commend my spirit' (Lk 23:46), and according to John his final words were, 'It is accomplished.' John adds immediately, 'and he bowed his head and gave up his spirit' (Jn 19:30). 'Accomplished', 'my spirit', 'his spirit' – in other words, my life, all that I am in the very depth of my being, all that I have aimed for throughout my life. His sacrifice is one of total surrender to the Father. In Christ's case 'spiritual sacrifice' expresses nothing less than that.

The Heavenly Sacrifice

Christ's sacrifice does not come to an abrupt end with his death on the cross. What we might call his sacrificial disposition and intent will endure in him, fixed eternally in that moment of accomplishment, of consummation, of complete surrender to the Father.

Christ offered himself once and for all, but that was no merely transient act of his. His offering endures in him, endures in him in heaven, just as the Father's acceptance of it in raising Jesus from the dead endures. That moment of surrender on Christ's part and of acceptance on the Father's has passed beyond our realm of space and time and continues forever in heaven. In that sense we may speak of the heavenly sacrifice, not a new sacrifice but Christ's single sacrifice made once for all by him and once for all accepted by the Father, this sacrifice living on in Christ glorified in the eternal now. The author of Hebrews says of Christ that because he continues forever he is able for all time to save those who draw near to God through him, since he always lives to make intercession for them (Heb 7:25). He is continuously pleading his once-for-all, but ever-living, sacrifice before God on our behalf. He can do that because he is indeed a priest but of a unique and permanent kind, with a sacrifice that transcends all others.

The Sacrifice of the Church

Up to this point we have been concerned primarily with Christ's sacrifice. As we have seen, the eucharist is the sacrament of that sacrifice. In its celebration of the memorial of what he said and did at the Last Supper, the Church is caught up into that mystery. Christ in the totality of his sacrifice becomes present in a unique way and he draws the Church into the depths of his sacrifice, so that this may work to accomplish his purpose in us and in our lives.

As Christ was the priest who offered his sacrifice and at the same time the victim, so is the Church, but always in imitation of Christ and in complete dependence on him. The Church, as the living body of Christ, is caught up in Christ's self-offering and at the same time it offers itself in the power of that sacrifice, and until the day of Christ's second coming it will have to go on striving to become in the entirety of its existence the sacrifice it offers. 'Church' here must be taken not just in its collective sense but as including the individual members who make up each and every eucharistic assembly, with due recognition of the distinctive role of the ordained priest. In that way Christ's sacrifice becomes the Church's, ours. Within the ritual of the eucharist we express this in the offering the priest, as minister of Christ and minister of the Church, makes after the institution narrative and consecration.[8]

The classical expression of this takes the form 'commemorating, we offer'. Our commemoration is of such depth and density as to give rise to an offering. By the gift and grace of Christ and by the power of the Holy Spirit, we can offer to the Father the sacrifice of Christ as our sacrifice. Several of our eucharistic prayers make clear that the offering we make to God is one that God has first given to us. As emphasised already, this must never be just an external or merely ritual offering. St Augustine says that in offering this to God the Church is learning to offer itself; we must ourselves become the sacrifice that we make – and that not just within the celebration of the eucharist but over the whole range of our lives.[9] As Christ's sacrifice made him what he was at the moment of his death, and now lives on in him in glory, so our sacrifice for us. It is to reach its culmination in our death and to endure in us for all eternity.

This is to be seen in Eucharistic Prayers III and IV, in their use of the language of sacrifice, offering, oblation after the institution narrative and consecration of the Mass. The different, though closely connected, levels of the eucharistic mystery emerge clearly.

In Eucharistic Prayer IV, as we celebrate the memorial of our redemption, we offer to God Christ's 'Body and Blood, the sacrifice acceptable to you which brings salvation to the whole world'. Next, in asking God to look with favour on our offering, we plead that it is the sacrifice that God himself has provided for his Church. Then we go on to pray that all who enter into it through their partaking of Christ's Body and Blood may themselves become a living sacrifice in Christ. In other words, we offer Christ's sacrifice as our own and we pray that by its grace we may become a similar sacrifice in ourselves and in our lives.

Similarly, and more extensively, in Eucharistic Prayer III. There, in the immediate context of our celebration of the memorial of Christ's passion, resurrection and ascension, and in the expectation of his second coming, we offer 'this holy and living sacrifice'. Then, having prayed that God will 'look ... upon the oblation of your Church', we go on a few lines later to pray that God may 'make of us an eternal offering to you, so that we may obtain an inheritance with your elect'. We have made our offering but we have still to become that offering in ourselves and in our lives. It is an oblation that in due time will bring us to glory, to its fulfilment there, and it will live on in us eternally. All of this, of course, will be the fruit of Christ's sacrifice at work in us. But the effect of the eucharistic sacrifice is not confined to those who participate in the particular celebration. Eucharistic Prayer III carries its theme of sacrifice and offering still further. 'May this Sacrifice of our reconciliation ... advance the peace and salvation of all the world.' This is not just a general prayer made on the occasion of a eucharistic celebration. It is rather a prayer from within the eucharist itself, asking that the effects of this celebration may extend to the ends of the earth. Such is the power and the reach and the purpose of the eucharistic mystery itself.

The Language of Sacrifice Today

The Jewish people of the Old Testament had a variety of sacrifices, all of them concerned with their relationship with God. This was a relationship that they had often damaged by sin, and many of their sacrifices tried to make expiation to God or sought forgiveness or reconciliation. They were rooted in an awareness, kept fresh and strong by the prophets, of their weakness and their sin.

For Christians, Christ's one sacrifice took up all of that into itself and accomplished what those sacrifices could never accomplish of themselves. In that sense, sin is at the heart of sacrifice. We recall why God gave Jesus his name through an angel before his birth: 'because he shall save his people from their sins' (Mt 1:21). We recall too his own words at the Last Supper, that his blood would be poured out 'for the forgiveness of sins' (Mt 26:28).

There is an important lesson for us in this, because the fact and the nature of sin are so often glossed over or ignored or denied altogether in our contemporary world. Sin is as much a reality of the present as it was of the past, and, left to ourselves, we are still unable to overcome it or its effects. We also need an acute awareness of the cost at which Christ in himself overcame our sin and its power – the cost to himself and indeed the cost to the Father, who gave us his beloved Son and in him reconciled our sinful world to himself. The reality of sin and the cost of our reconciliation are displayed plainly in the figure of Christ on his cross, suspended there in love and in agony between heaven and earth, and with arms outstretched to embrace the whole world.

We use many words to convey our understanding of Christ and his life, but the word 'sacrifice' has a privileged place among them. While only partially, of course, it encapsulates in a very special way so much of what we believe to be the heart of this. To allow the word 'sacrifice' to drop quietly from our regular Christian vocabulary would lead to an enormous loss to us. It would weaken our grasp of the great mystery of Christ in all its fullness, a mystery that is the core of our faith; it would weaken too the understanding of faith that we bring to the celebration of the eucharist in memory of him. As a result, it would weaken our understanding of all that the mystery of Christ and our participation in the eucharist should mean to us, what they bring to us and what they demand of us. If Christ's death on the cross is a great sacrifice, then the eucharist is a great sacrifice because of its relationship to the cross, and we who participate in the eucharist, we, in the entirety of our being and our lives, are to become a great sacrifice too.

The decline of the word and the weakening and narrowing of faith go together; the influence is reciprocal, and we are much the poorer for both. It is not just the gradual disappearance of a word; it is the effect on faith that this disappearance both indicates and hastens.

4

The Presence of Christ

In the pages that follow, while reference will be made occasionally to Christ's presence in the Church and in the liturgy as a whole, it is principally his presence in the eucharist that is the focus of attention.

Of the many important articles in *Sacrosanctum Concilium*, the Constitution on the Liturgy issued by the Second Vatican Council, one of the more influential has proved to be article 7, on the different forms that the presence of Christ takes in the Church's liturgy. It is of interest to recall that Pope Pius XII had already spoken of several of these in his encyclical *Mediator Dei* in 1947, but this passed largely unnoticed at the time or in the years after. When the Second Vatican Council, however, presented the same teaching in a somewhat more developed form in 1963, it attracted a great deal of attention and interest. And since then it has entered very easily into our thinking and our speaking about liturgical celebration. Pope Paul VI took it up in his encyclical *Mysterium Fidei* issued shortly after the Council. There he developed it and extended it beyond the liturgy to the wider life of the Church.

This was happening at a time when it seemed that the word 'presence' was beginning to enjoy a fresh vitality in public discourse more generally. We were using it with a broader reference and in a more personal, more subjective way. For Catholics then it was as if this article was a teaching, an expression of truth, whose time had come. Why should this have been so?

Real Presence

One of the effects of the eucharistic controversies of the sixteenth century was that the Catholic Church had to place very heavy emphasis on its teaching that Christ becomes truly, really and substantially present in his body and blood in the celebration of the eucharist. 'The Real Presence' became the name increasingly used by Catholics to express the Catholic position. 'Real' in order to bring out the true depth and density of Christ's presence in the eucharistic species. This title served the Church well in distinguishing its position from what it regarded as the inadequate designations of the Reformers (a dynamic presence, a virtual presence, a symbolic presence), and also in bringing home to its members the substantial nature of Christ's true presence.

But as we look back we can see that the emphatic and exclusive use of the title 'The Real Presence' brought loss too.

Christ is present when the Christian people gathers and prays in his name; he is present when the scriptures are read there; he is present in the priest, because he himself is the true minister of the sacraments. We have always believed this, but in the years since the Second Vatican Council we have come to emphasise the distinct nature of each, while recognising the particular role it plays within the totality of, say, the eucharist.

But if the real presence of Christ is in the bread and wine now transformed in their very substance into Christ's true body and blood, how are we to characterise those other forms of his presence? Are they somehow not real, less than real? No one would say that, but what other word is to be used for them to convey what the Church recognises as distinctive in them and to retain the full content that Christian faith finds in them?

Article 7 of the Constitution on the Liturgy has been very helpful here. Instead of speaking simply of Christ's presence in the eucharist and other sacraments, it spoke rather of different forms that this presence takes. At the end of the gospel according to St Matthew, as Jesus was taking leave of his disciples for the last time, he said: 'Behold, I am with you always, even to the end of the age' (Mt 28:20). No qualifications here, no terms and conditions. He is present at all times and everywhere in his Church. There is no activity of the Church done in his name, no situation of its true life, from which he is absent. While by Christ's grace the Church universal will never forfeit his presence, in its concrete manifestations it may well fail to recognise its Lord present in a particular way or may ignore it or may thwart his purpose. But even there he will still be present, enlightening his people, calling them back to faithfulness.

Christ thus adapts himself to the particular situation and to the appropriate means to be used there for the accomplishment of his purpose. His presence to his Church takes many forms.

This was what article 7 of the Constitution on the Liturgy achieved for us. It showed us how to speak of Christ's presence in the Church and at the same time to acknowledge the many different ways in which this presence is realised.

Presences?

Some commentators spoke and perhaps still speak of Christ's 'presences' in the liturgy. This, I think is mistaken. There is no partial presence of Christ, as if as a rule he was not fully present or as if there were areas of the Church from which he was absent. There is one, undivided Christ and he is present in all his fullness, always and everywhere to his Church over the whole range of its life and its activities – a single, all-embracing presence. Having acknowledged this truth, we can then go on to speak of different forms that this presence takes.

The Christ who is Present

What does it mean to say that Christ is present in our liturgical celebrations? On the feast of Christmas we speak of Christ 'born for us this day' or we sing: 'Today a Saviour has been born for us: he is Christ the Lord.' The liturgy is doing more here than just echoing the message of the angels on the first Christmas night. 'Today' is the today of each feast of the Nativity. How are we to understand this liturgical 'today'?

Jesus was born once only, at a particular time and in a particular place. This is an event of history that cannot be repeated. Neither can it be rerun, as we might replay a recording or a video. But on the annual celebration of his nativity does Jesus himself somehow revert for our sake to his state of infancy? Sometimes we have spoken of Christmas as if this were indeed the case. But this does not seem any more plausible than repetition in the here and now of the historical event of his birth. But we still cannot allow the great feast of Christmas to be reduced to little more than a commemoration, much as on each Easter Monday the Irish state commemorates the 1916 Rising or as Britain commemorates VE day each year on 8 May.

When we celebrate the Lord's passion on Good Friday, we certainly believe, and we feel, that we are doing much more than merely remembering an event of importance for us from the past. We believe that what took place then is brought very close to us and we to it.

Christ died once, on that day on Calvary, and this cannot be repeated. The Church's liturgical action on Good Friday, however understood, cannot be any sort of rerun of that singular event. What then can we say about the 'content' of our liturgical memorial?

What we have at Christmas and on Good Friday is not the presence of a free-floating, disembodied mystery, so to speak, one that can become contemporaneous with us through the liturgy. It is the presence of the person who in himself lived that mystery, and it is in that presence that we are given our answer. The original event of the nativity can be present for us of later times only if in some sense it has remained present in Christ. But surely this is indeed the case? The great mysteries of Christ's incarnate life break out of all the limitations of space and time and in the glorified humanity of the unique person of Christ, Son of God, live on eternally.

Through the presence of Christ there, the liturgy of the Nativity or of Good Friday is a sort of sacrament of the original mystery.

Neither Christ nor his life can be compartmentalised. It is the one Christ in the entirety of his being who is present, and that Christ is now risen and glorified with the Father. But the great mysteries of his life on earth live on in him now in his glory. And so, when we celebrate the feast of the Nativity, Christ does not somehow revert to his infancy. It is not a new-born babe who is present but the glorified Lord, in whom the mystery of his birth is still a living reality. This is the infant who lived his life faithfully through to the end and is now with the Father in glory. In that state of glory his birth has reached its fulfilment and will always be living in him.

Similarly on Good Friday, it is not as if Christ relived in himself all the agony of the cross. In his death his whole life was recapitulated and ratified, and it was precisely by and through his death that he passed over into glory. That moment of final surrender, now irrevocable on his part, is met by the Father's total and immediate acceptance of it in the resurrection. In his passing into glory, Christ's life and death are utterly transformed. He has passed beyond space and time and that moment lives on in him in the eternal now. And so, even on Good Friday, it is this Lord, now risen and glorified, who is present to us in all the mysteries of his life. Is this part of the truth that he shows to his disciples in the fact that in his risen body he still retained the wounds in his hands and his side?

So too for other mysteries of his public ministry that we celebrate, notably his baptism and his transfiguration.

Christ's Presence in the Eucharist

It is at Christ's summons that the Church gathers for the eucharist, and when it responds in faith Christ is present as he promised. Individual Christians, families, other small groups all make their way by their own paths and converge on their place of unity, and with the priest they form the one liturgical assembly. This is the body of Christ come together here and now, and Christ is there as its head, there to lead it in faith as its true priest and to bring its prayers and its offerings to the Father. Two or three have gathered in his name and he is there among them (Mt 18:20).

Christ's disciples must be called constantly to faith; they must be called to repentance. And so they must hear the gospel as proclaimed originally by Christ; they must be instructed, as Christ instructed his first disciples; they must be nourished by his teaching. Only Christ himself can do this, if now through the ministry of those who read the scripture and who preach on it in his name. 'You are not to be called "rabbi",' Jesus said, 'for you have only one teacher ... you have only one master, Christ' (Mt 23:8-10). If we Christians are to hear Christ's word, it must be he who proclaims it to us and so in some sense he must be present in that word when it is proclaimed. In this way the word of God becomes 'something alive and active' in the eucharistic assembly (Heb 4:12-13).

Similarly he must be present too in us who hear it; to open our ears and our minds and our hearts and to draw a response from us. Otherwise we will be listening to just some ancient text, with whatever interest, if any, such a text may have for us.

Christ is present in the priest, his ordained minister, who is to preside over the eucharistic assembly in his name and to lead it in prayer and in its celebration of the Lord's word. It is the priest who will proclaim the eucharistic prayer, who will pray for the Holy Spirit to come on the bread and wine, and who, in imitation of Christ's own actions at the Last Supper, will take the bread and wine and in Christ's name will pronounce over them Christ's own words. In this regard there are two *dicta* long in use in our tradition, two complementary expressions of a single truth: The priest acts *in persona Christi*, in the person of Christ; Christ acts *in persona ministri*, in the person of the minister. The second of these is the more fundamental: it places the emphasis on Christ rather than on his minister; but it is useful for us to have both expressions in speaking about this truth.

The Christ who is already present in his assembled brothers and sisters, the Christ who has shared his word with us, the Christ who has been present in the essential actions and words of the priest, is now present *par excellence* in the very substance of his body and blood. We say that after the institution narrative and consecration of the Mass, Christ is present or present in a unique way. This of course is true. But in order to understand this truth more fully and to arrive at a more nuanced statement of the Church's faith, we must keep in mind both the context and the form that Christ chose in giving us this gift of himself.

Christ has given us this surpassing form of his presence not just to be with us. 'Take and eat,' he said, 'take and drink.' His intent is to unite his Church even more closely with himself and in itself: 'grant ... to all who partake of this one Bread and one Chalice that, gathered into one body by the Holy Spirit ...' So Eucharistic Prayer IV, and our other post-Vatican II eucharistic prayers make the same petition in similar words. Christ is present in his body and blood, so that we, accepting his invitation, following his command, may receive that presence in the most personal and intimate way. By responding in faith and love, we allow Christ to work his great purpose in the depths of our lives and our being, as Church and as individual Christians. We are the body of Christ and we receive the body of Christ in order to become all the more the body of Christ. And so we can be sent out from the eucharistic assembly of God's people strengthened in ourselves and among ourselves, strengthened too to announce the gospel of the Lord, to bear witness to him, to glorify him by our lives. We brought our lives to the eucharist and now we are sent forth to bring the eucharist to our lives in the world about us.

With the Father, in and by the Holy Spirit
Up to this point we have been concerned with the person of Christ and his presence to us and among us. We have seen something of the range and the power of what Christ does there.

But there is a further dimension to this presence. The mystery of the eucharist is a mystery of Christ, but not understood in any narrow or exclusive way. It is a mystery of the whole Trinity, as our eucharistic prayers make very clear. Here I am concerned with just an aspect of this, what this will mean when we speak of the presence of Christ.

It is especially in the gospel of St John that Jesus speaks of his relationship to the Father and of the intimacy of this relationship. He and the Father are one, he says: the Father is in him and he is in the Father (Jn 10:30, 38, 14:10-11, 20). It is a truth he comes back to again and again. Just as it is always in Christ that we meet the Father, so it is always the Father who brings us to Christ. 'No one can come to me unless the Father who sent me draws him' (Jn 6:44). There is no need to multiply texts. Jesus' own words are clear and they place it beyond dispute. Christ and his Father are inseparable. We will continue to distinguish, as we must, between the roles of Christ and of his Father in accomplishing the great divine plan for our salvation. But the truth is even deeper and richer.

Christ promised that when he returned to the Father he would send the Holy Spirit upon his disciples (Jn 16:7). In and by the Spirit he would remain with them and would guide them. The Spirit would continue Christ's ministry here on earth until all was completed in accordance with the Father's will.

At first sight this might seem to be some sort of presence by delegation or proxy, as if Christ were now providing for his Church through his Spirit, while he remained in heaven until all is fulfilled. But this is not the case. It is not as if Christ has to be distant, absent, while the Holy Spirit completes the ministry that first brought Christ into the world. There is a lot here that we cannot understand, but in speaking about the work of realising God's plan for the world and for our salvation, can we go so far as to say that where Christ, the glorified Lord, is present and active, there the Spirit is, and where the Spirit is present and active, there Christ is; what the one does, the other does equally. Such is the degree of unity and of cooperation between them, to put it in crude human terms, such is that unity of purpose and cooperation in perfect harmony in advancing the divine plan of salvation and bringing it to the fulfilment that is the Father's will. But again, while we acknowledge this and recognise how inadequate our attempts to express and to understand it are, we will continue to distinguish the roles of Christ and of his Spirit, guided throughout by the Spirit and by Christ's own words and the truth they reveal.

Reciprocal Presence

Someone may be present in a room alone. Someone may be present in a crowded carriage of a commuter train or on a busy street of some great city, but still have no communication with those all around. Generally, however, the word 'presence' suggests something more than merely the proximity of others. Presence is personal, not just in the sense that it involves me in a personal way but also in the sense that it involves others. Presence as a rule is interpersonal and reciprocal. My response to others invites a response, their presence to me. This can go from little more than mere acknowledgment to some form of engagement with me right up to moments of great intimacy between us.

Christ is present in the Church not simply to be there. His is an active presence that seeks an active response, that invites us to engage with him in the way that is appropriate. The heart of this will always be faith, when the desire of Christ to be with us is met by our desire to be present to him. When this takes place, there is a genuine encounter, the presence is mutual, and in that sense is fulfilled.

Thus when we gather on a Sunday for the eucharist in the communion of the whole Church, our first response should be our recognition of the person of Christ calling us together, of his presence among us and in us, of what we are by Christ's grace and what we are to one another, his body. This has clear implications for how we regard our fellow members of the body and how we treat one another both in church and outside it.

How are we to respond in faith to Christ present to us and speaking to us in his word? We listen to the readings and we engage with them. This is not then a merely passive listening on our part but must be active; we open ourselves in the power of the Holy Spirit and we listen for what the Lord may have to say to us. It would be a mistake, however, to expect an instant, easily identifiable effect on every occasion. Far more often the process is a slow one; the Lord may wish to work on us imperceptibly over time in order to make us ready to receive what he has to say to us. So, an important part of our response to the Lord's presence in his word is patience and perseverance, an ear ever open and attuned to the sound of his voice.

How do we respond to Christ's presence in his priest? We respond by recognising that through his minister Christ is leading us into the very depths of the mystery of his own life, death and resurrection, that he is using the words and actions of his minister to make himself present to us, present truly, really and substantially in his very body and blood, with all that that means for us and brings to us.

This is the form of his presence *par excellence*. How are we to respond to it? In faith that will express itself in a combination of wonder, thanksgiving, praise, worship, love, petition. This is the beginning of our response, but we must prolong it and deepen it by taking that body, taking that blood, as he commanded us, and in that act entering into communion with the Lord in his life, death and resurrection. Then we devote our own lives to living out faithfully, as the Church and as its individual members, what the Lord desires to accomplish in and through us, the purpose he had in giving the eucharist to his Church. The Church makes the eucharist, but the eucharist too makes the Church. Again, we have two complementary statements of a single truth; and again, it is the second that is the more fundamental.

gathered to remember

5

In Christ

When St Paul encountered Jesus on the road to Damascus, he fell to the ground and asked: 'Who are you, Lord?' Jesus' response taught him a lesson that would remain with him for the rest of his life and become one of his deepest convictions and insights of faith: 'I am Jesus and you are persecuting me' (Acts 9:3-5). Jesus identifies himself in a double way here: he does so in a personal way by disclosing his name and he identifies himself too with his followers and them with himself. It is a truth that keeps on recurring in one form or another throughout Paul's letters, keeps on recurring not just because it is an important truth in itself but because it is at the heart of all Paul's thoughts and understanding, and because it claims its place in so many of the issues he deals with.

'In Christ' is a phrase that Paul uses frequently. At its broadest it expresses the relationship of Christians to Christ. To speak of Christians at any depth for Paul involves speaking about Christ. From Christ, Christians as Christians take their name and their belief and much of their way of life. But it goes much deeper than that. Their relationship is not with a figure of the distant past, a brilliant teacher, a powerful leader long since dead; it is a relationship of the present with the living Christ, a relationship that involves Christ's active presence to them, his living within them, and his ceaseless working in their lives – a total relationship, we might say. At this profound level, in Paul's understanding, we cannot think 'Christian' without thinking 'Christ'. It is from this relationship that Christians draw their true identity, their true existence, and their true life.

God Chose Us in Christ

For all of us this began in our baptism, but in God's plan it goes back long before our coming into being, long before the incarnation, long before anything actually existed; it goes back even before time, to God's intention in creating all that is. Already then, Paul says, God had chosen us in Christ (Eph 1:4).

All of this far transcends our understanding and our experience. And so we may well be inclined to leave Paul to his theological imagination and speculation. But for Paul this is no mere exercise in his own head. He is clear, definite and insistent in what he says. It shows the depths at which he is working, as he struggles to open up the full truth as he understands it and to bring us closer to it. To our way of thinking, of course, existence of this kind for us, outside of the dimensions of the world, is no existence at all. But can we say the same about God, about the power and the effectiveness of God's thought, design, intention? Do we not have to say rather that already in some mysterious but real way we have true existence in God, even before we were born? And that existence in God is already an existence in Christ.

God 'chose us in Christ before the world was made to be holy and faultless before him in love, marking us out beforehand, to be his adopted children through Jesus Christ'. In this way, 'he has blessed us with all the spiritual blessings of heaven in Christ'. So St Paul says at the beginning of his letter to the Church in Ephesus (Eph 1:3-4). This truth is developed more fully in the letter to the Colossians: Christ is 'the first-born of all creation, for in him were created all things in heaven and on earth ... all things were created through him and for him ... in him all things hold together' (Col 1:15-17).

That is how close and how fundamental our relationship to Christ is. In this sense we have always been 'in Christ'. There is something very encouraging and reassuring, I find, in this truth, because it means that Christ is always there in ourselves, present in us and for us. At this basic level, we never have to go looking for an absent and elusive Christ, we do not have to strive and strain for his attention, because he is already within us as we are within him, in some fundamental and objective sense. We may not recognise this, we may reject him, we may be living a life of serious sin, but even in these circumstances God has made us his own in Christ. Even as we are disowning Christ and trying to extricate ourselves from him, we are still anchored in him in an unbreakable relationship and with complete security.

But of course God has made us for a much closer and more intimate relationship with Christ than this. In the face of the universal sinfulness of the human race, Christ as the head of all creation, and more specifically as the head of humanity, came on earth as one of us, lived our life, died our death, and so redeemed us. And in doing so, he united us to himself in a completely new way, a union with him in the present that is a call to and a promise of an even closer union with him in the world to come. It is this that engages Paul in a large part of his writings, where he strives to understand it in its depths and in its many aspects, and to share his understanding with his fellow disciples. It is in this context that he uses frequently his phrase 'in Christ'. For Paul, 'in Christ' is not a passing, occasional truth, to be renewed in us from time to time. This may be how we are inclined to think of it, becoming aware of it only on special religious occasions and ignoring it otherwise. But this would be an error, a gross failure on our part. Even in our lack of advertence and appreciation the great truth remains, not as something to be left in God's safe keeping when we are not thinking about it, but as a truth for each of us and all of us, a truth of the here and now, a truth of every moment. We are 'in Christ' simply as an enduring fact of our existence. If all that I have been saying, following St Paul, is true, then it is a truth of the greatest possible importance for us and merits our total and whole-hearted response. It is in Christ that we celebrate every eucharist, just as it is in Christ that we exist at every moment as Christians. This is a living truth for all of us to bring to every eucharistic assembly. It is a wonderful truth to begin the Mass with, but what flows from it is much richer and still more wonderful.

'In Christ' expresses Christ's total, global, foundational relationship with us, and ours with him, in any or all of its dimensions.

And so, this truth goes to the very root of our being, what makes us what we are. It gives us our *raison d'être*, just as it gives us in a broad sense our goal and our map of life; it identifies where true happiness and our personal fulfilment are to be found; it gives us the strength and encouragement that we need for our journey and the bread of life to bring us there.

This is the reality of our daily, routine life, but it is a hidden truth, open only to faith and to a strong desire to take it to heart and to engage it.

Christ, Christians and the Eucharist

It is in Christ then that we celebrate the eucharist. It is his gift of love to his followers and it is in obedience to his command, in acceptance of his invitation, that we celebrate it in union with him and in his power. We are never alone, as a people or as individuals, in doing so. It is he who has gathered us around him, and, in accordance with his promise, he is there, present and active in our midst. It is his gospel that is proclaimed there, and, as *Sacrosanctum Concilium*, the Constitution on the Liturgy (7) reminds us, he is present because it is his word that is present in his proclamation of his gospel and in the people who hear it. He is present in the person and the ministerial action of the ordained priest, who acts in his name. And, as a climax, he is present in the sacramental bread and wine, which have become by divine power his body and blood. All of this is of divine doing and we must say that Christ is the principal actor in the eucharist, the main celebrant.

We shall return to all of this later under different aspects, and in particular to the demands that it makes of us. We join with Christ in celebrating the eucharist and we shall have to examine what this means for us. But for now it is mainly the role of Christ that concerns us, in what sense we must say that it is always in Christ that we approach it and engage with it and exercise our true role there.

As Christ is the first in the order of creation, so he is first too in the new creation, in his resurrection the first of an immense company of brothers and sisters to be born in accordance with the great divine design (Rm 8:29). In everything that flows from this, he it is who takes first place and who makes it possible for us to participate in all its blessings. There is no blessing of this kind that does not come to us from our relationship to Christ. It is because we are in him that, already in this world, we have begun to share in the great blessings of the world to come.

'In Christ' – I have emphasised this very strongly right from the beginning because it is important that we do not reduce or undervalue its truth. Our human tendency is to place ourselves and our human efforts at the centre and to relate everything else to them. Especially since the Second Vatican Council, we have placed great emphasis on the eucharist as our celebration, the celebration of this congregation gathered in this Church here today. Of course there is an important truth in this and it was a blessing of the Council and its aftermath to have brought this to the fore again for us. But it is not the whole truth, not even the central truth, of the eucharist, and in retrieving a truth not sufficiently recognised in recent years, we must not thereby ignore or pass over too lightly other great truths of our tradition. It is for this reason that I have chosen to place this chapter, 'In Christ', towards the beginning. From the outset it places Christ at the centre, and ourselves in our true relationship with him.

The Holy Spirit, the Giver of Life

Whenever we say the Nicene Creed, we profess our belief in the Holy Spirit, the Lord, the Giver of life. There were many titles the Council could have given the Spirit: the Spirit of Love, the Spirit of Wisdom, the sanctifying Spirit, the enlightening Spirit, the unifying Spirit, all of which shed their light on an important aspect of the Spirit or of the Spirit's work, but 'the Giver of Life' is the one chosen, and what this title denotes has deep roots in scripture.

The Christian doctrine of the Holy Spirit is not, of course, explicit in the Old Testament, but the Christian tradition, rereading the Old Testament in the light of Christ and his message, has been able to find foreshadowings and anticipations of its own, later doctrine of the Holy Spirit.

Thus, in the very opening verses of the book of Genesis (Gn 1:2), which speak of the wind or the breath or the spirit moving or hovering over the primeval waters, Christians recognise the Holy Spirit, the breath of God, the breath of life. And as we learn a few verses later (Gn 2:7), it is that breath or spirit that gives life to Adam when God breathes into his nostrils. Another strand in Christian tradition sees here an image, charming and homely, of a mother hen, brooding over her nest, as she brings forth her new life and nurtures its beginnings. However we may understand the figure, Christian tradition recognises that God's Spirit is life-giving, and is already present and active, right from the start, in God's act of creation.

Some chapters later in Genesis (Gn 8:11), in the account of the flood, when the waters have cleared sufficiently from the face of the earth, the dove returns to Noah with an olive branch in its beak, a sign to Noah that life is beginning again on earth. Again, it is a favourite image for Christians: the dove, the Holy Spirit, the Spirit of life, draws life from death.

There is no need to multiply instances: God's Spirit is creative and life-giving. And through the rest of scripture we will learn that this Spirit is ceaselessly active in the world.

From the very beginning of the New Testament the Spirit is there. It is the Spirit who gives life to the humanity of Jesus in Mary's womb (Mt 1:20; Lk 1:35), and all through Jesus' life the Spirit remains with him to shape and guide and direct that life, to bring it to death and through death to resurrection and through resurrection to full life with the Father in glory. And again, at the beginnings of the Church, it is the same Spirit who descends on Pentecost day (Acts 2:4) and transforms the disciples, giving new vitality to them, to their preaching, to their witness. And so it continues down through the centuries and will continue, until, at the end, the Spirit, with Christ, will have brought God's great plan for the world to fulfilment, to that new life with God that is the new creation: the new heavens and the new earth and the new humanity.

The Holy Spirit in the Eucharist

I have remarked several times in these pages what a blessing for us the eucharistic prayers introduced after the Second Vatican Council have been. It is the blessing of a better awareness of the role of the Holy Spirit, especially in the eucharist, that concerns me here. The Roman Canon, the single eucharistic prayer in use in the Roman Rite for centuries and now Eucharistic Prayer I, makes no mention of the Holy Spirit, apart from being included with the Father and the Son in the final doxology. Even at the time of the Second Vatican Council, we knew that our pneumatology, that is, our theology of the Spirit, was weak. But the Council developed its understanding as it went along, and in a later document a wonderful expression is used of the Spirit. Dealing with the eucharist, it speaks of it as 'given life and giving life by the Holy Spirit'.[10] The new eucharistic prayers of the years following have made us a lot more familiar with the fact that the Spirit is indeed present and active in the eucharist, and they have helped us to grow in our understanding of his work there. In this respect we owe a great deal to the Churches of the East. They have always had a much stronger awareness than we of the Spirit in the Church in general, and in particular in the unfolding of the eucharist.

The Spirit, as we have seen, has been active in the world right from the beginning, but at Pentecost the Spirit came in a special way on the early disciples. Eucharistic Prayer IV says that the Spirit was sent by Christ in glory from the Father 'so that, bringing to perfection his (Christ's) work in the world, he might sanctify creation to the full'. 'Perfect' is a word that tradition uses widely of the work of the Spirit, a word that in this context links the Spirit very closely to Jesus. The action of the Spirit is not a parallel mission, running alongside that of Jesus; it is a mission, so to speak, that is the fruit of Christ's own, working ceaselessly to bring it to the completion that has always been God's intention. And that will not be until the end of time.

This then is the Spirit invoked immediately after in what we know technically as the first *epiclesis*. In the fulfilment of the Spirit's mission as just presented in Eucharistic Prayer IV, he is to come down on the bread and wine to make of them the body and blood of Christ, a life-giving work indeed. Eucharistic Prayers II and III have a similar invocation of the Spirit at this point, praying for the same effect, and, while they do not place the prayer in the fuller context that Eucharistic Prayer IV does, it is on the same truth that they are drawing.

This is continued after the institution narrative and consecration in the second *epiclesis*, which prays that all of those who partake of Christ's body and blood may be filled with the Holy Spirit and become one body, one spirit in Christ. All three eucharistic prayers, while using slightly differing expressions, agree on what they are seeking from God. By the sanctifying working of the Spirit, Christ's one eucharistic body is to unite those who receive it so as to make of them the one ecclesial body of Christ. As is clear, this is not a new, additional, work of the Holy Spirit. It is a dimension of the Spirit's activity in the world from the beginning and what, as the Spirit of God, the Holy Spirit has been doing in the Church from the day of Pentecost.

One can see what the Second Vatican Council meant in saying of the eucharist that it is given life and gives life by the Holy Spirit. It is the Spirit who, in the consecration, brings Christ's words of the Last Supper alive and into the present, so that they achieve in *this* eucharist what they achieved when Christ first spoke them. Thus, by the power of life at work in the Holy Spirit, Christ's words give an utterly new life and power to the natural gifts of bread and wine, so that these are thereby empowered to give the same Spirit to those who partake of them. We could say of the Holy Spirit that the Spirit is at once the cause and the fruit of Christ's presence in his body and blood.

As we saw earlier, according to Eucharistic Prayer IV, Christ sent the gift of the Spirit from the Father 'so that, bringing to perfection his (Christ's) work in the world, he might sanctify creation to the full'. This, of course, is not confined to the eucharist, though in the eucharist we see a very telling instance of it. That work began with creation and it must go on until the end of time, but we have a sacrament of it, as it were, in the eucharist. Each eucharist is celebrated at a particular point in the evolving of God's plan. The whole salvific movement up to the present is somehow there and is celebrated there. In the eucharist we are drawn into that movement where it is now, and we are sent out to continue in it and to work faithfully there in order to carry it onwards into God's future. The eucharist celebrates that divine work of the past and it looks forward in anticipation to its consummation, when God's project will be completed.

The Holy Spirit is active all through this time, working on the divine project to advance it throughout history, with all its human weakness and sin, and, in spite of the resistance and rejection that the Spirit meets from us all the time. But that goal of God's, and in God's own good time, will be attained by the ceaseless work of the Holy Spirit. Every time we celebrate the eucharist, we are given an assurance of that in the gift of Christ's body and blood. And not just an assurance but that future itself present even now to us in sacrament in Christ. And so we go out from the Mass to work for it, to cooperate with the Spirit in bringing the mystery at the heart of the eucharist into our own lives, into the life of the Church and the life of the wider world. The mystery we celebrate in the eucharist is to be the mystery of the rest of our lives, given life and giving life by the Holy Spirit.

Remember

Remember: it is one of the great, seminal words of the Old Testament; a lot of Jewish history is represented there. It is God's word of command to his people, to keep fresh in their minds, and to keep as a powerful influence in their lives, all that God has done for them throughout their history, all that God has said to them and imposed on them: the exodus from Egypt, the great covenant made with them through Moses on Mount Sinai and the Law that accompanied it, support of them in their forty long and difficult years in the wilderness, the gift to them of the promised land, and so on down through the centuries.

During all that time, God had shown himself to be their God, faithful to the people of the covenant, God-with-them. So in remembering the wonders that God had done for them, they were remembering not just deeds of a rapidly receding past but they were being reminded all the time of their God of the present. Through all that God has done and said, God has been revealing himself as a God who loves the people, God is faithful to them from generation to generation; what God has promised to do God does and will go on doing. A God to be trusted then, always.

The Law that God gave them through Moses continues to hold good, because God's words are words of enduring validity, spoken to them for their lasting good, words of life then, words to sustain them in the present, words for them to live by into the future.

When you read parts of the Old Testament, you have to be struck by the frequency of 'remember' and of variants of it. It is a constant reminder to God's people of the nature of their God and of God's demand for their faithful response.

This should not be taken to suggest that God's 'remember' was to be heard just as a stern warning or a severe threat, imposing an obligation to be kept with grim determination. No doubt there were times when this was indeed so, but it was also, and primarily, a source of joy, a memory to be treasured, a memory to give rise to thanksgiving and praise and blessing of God. In the psalms, for example, God is often thanked and praised by acknowledging or recounting before God some of the wonderful deeds God has done for the people. The memory itself, identified and lit up from within by faith and love and joy, becomes a blessing of God.

But there is another side to it. 'Remember' is not just God's frequently repeated word to the people. It is their word to God too. It is the people's ongoing plea to God in their experience of failure, weakness, hardship, suffering, need: Lord, remember your mighty deeds of the past; remember how faithful you have always proved yourself to be; remember how frail we are and have been always; remember how much help we have always needed; remember your mercies and your love of the past; remember that this is the sort of God you are; and, as you remember, be with us, forgive us, strengthen us, grant us what you know we need.

In their mutual remembering of the past, God and God's people meet in the present and prepare for the future.

This is a memory that must be kept alive and made its own by every succeeding generation and passed on faithfully as a living truth to the next.

This is the very rich background that the Old Testament provides for the memory or memorial of the New. And it is more than mere background: it is a contributory part of the New, while being transcended by it.

The Memorial of the Eucharist

At the Last Supper, according to Paul and Luke, after Jesus had pronounced his words of thanksgiving over the bread and over the wine he added: 'Do this in memory of me' or 'Do this as a memorial of me' (1 Cor 11:24-25; Lk 22:19). Who is to remember him? The long Christian tradition has interpreted Jesus' words as meaning: Do this so that you may remember me, so that the memory of me may always be renewed and kept fresh and strong by the eucharist. But there have been voices too to argue that it is the Father who is to be reminded. In this interpretation, what Christ's words would mean is: do this so that the Father may remember me and all that I have done and all that God has done through me – and that, remembering, the Father may give effect to it in the present, for the good of the Church and of the world and of the people who observe this memorial in Christ's name here and now. Whatever may have been the Lord's intent when he spoke those words first, the eucharist is surely large enough to embrace both interpretations. It is important to realise too that 'memory' is not just a subjective act here, a state of heightened consciousness, and that 'memorial' is a lot more than the sort of pageant of commemoration that the state, say, or smaller civic groups may put on at an anniversary to keep fresh and alive in the community the memory of the original event. I have dealt with this at greater length earlier in chapters three and four. The eucharist is a memorial of such objectivity and depth as to unite us who commemorate it with the original event itself, so that it brings the past somehow into the present for us here and now and enables it to exert its power on us today.

The Jewish people, celebrating the feast of Passover, for example, and recounting, and in some way re-enacting, the events of that great night of liberation, did not believe that their celebration was just a subjective remembering of an event of importance from their past. They believed that God was close to them, acting on them tonight, as they kept the Passover in accordance with God's commands, so close to them as to bring the original great deed of liberation into the present for this people and this family and its life.

But as a ritual of memorial, the eucharist goes far beyond even this. It has two unique features: it comes directly from Christ himself, chosen by him and given by him with the command to do it in his memory; it makes present to us through all ages the person of Christ in all the fullness of his mystery, present truly, really and substantially in his body and blood. This cannot be the effect of human power, not of human memory, not of human ritual. It can only be the effect of divine power – the power of God coming as the Holy Spirit upon the bread and wine, and achieving its effect through the proclamation of Christ's own words. Christ's is a living word, spoken once by him and now spoken in the eucharist by his ordained minister in his name and at his command, and given life in the present by the Spirit.

This is what places the memorial of the eucharist on a level all its own, a level for which we struggle to find the thoughts and the words, a level that in fact lies far beyond the range of our thoughts and our words, even the very best. All of this is God's gift to us, given in every celebration of the eucharist, and it is given to us so that we of every time may remember, in the strongest possible sense of that word, something of the great mystery Christ was in himself and that he lived – and, remembering this, may engage fully with him.

Of what is it a memorial? Given the fact that it was Christ who used the word, given the context in which he used it, it has to be a memorial of Christ himself, and more specifically of the great offering of his death on Calvary and of his anticipation of this at the Last Supper. 'Do this … ,' Jesus said: keep this ritual faithfully, it has the power to prolong through all time and for all the people yet to come the unique sacrifice that I shall consummate tomorrow and that I am making in a sacramental way here among you tonight. And we, two thousand years later, can bear witness with all the generations in between to the truth of that.

But, as we have seen in chapter three, Christ's death is not to be treated as if it were an isolated act of his. It is his most important single act, yes; a unique act, never done before and never to be done again, yes; but an act that was foreseen by God and was already in preparation in Christ's conception and birth, an act towards which his whole life was directed, an act that summed up and recapitulated that life and was its culmination on the cross. It is significant that according to St John's gospel Jesus' last words were: 'It is accomplished' (Jn 19:30).

But we believe that Jesus rose from the dead and began, so to speak, a new life, not a mere continuation or prolongation of the life that had been his before but now as that life utterly transformed, glorified, beyond all the laws of physics and chemistry, beyond all the limitations of space and time. 'Memory', 'memorial' may be words that we use with reference to the past, but in the case of the eucharist it is a remembrance of the ever-living and glorified Christ and of all that we mean by the event of Christ, a memorial then that unites past, present and future.

We can push still further back. There is an important sense in which the story of Christ does not begin with the Annunciation but in fact goes back to the beginning of all things in God's act of creation. St Paul can speak of Christ as being with the Father from the outset, he can say that all things exist through him and for him, even though his coming in the flesh as one like us is far into the future at this stage (Col 1:15-20). And when God's appointed time does come, the incarnation is itself the culmination of God's work from the very outset, of making all of creation ready for Christ to come. Eucharistic Prayer IV, together with the great eucharistic prayers of the Eastern tradition on which it is modelled, recalls in thanksgiving and praise this long history of God's preparing the way for Christ's coming.

'The fullness of time,' St Paul calls it in a memorable phrase (Gal 4:4). This could refer simply to Mary's time in accordance with God's plan. But Paul seems to have a bigger picture in mind: not just Mary's time as a mother but the time of her people too and the time the world has been waiting for and preparing for from the beginning.

The whole world, and then more particularly the Jewish people, had to be brought to the point at which Mary could be born as a worthy Mother of God's Son. The slow, patient and painstaking work of God that went into the making of Christ is indeed one of the marvels of God and is not to be forgotten or passed over. It lives on in the person of Christ, in his incarnate life, and in his cross and resurrection, and it is recalled in summary form in the eucharist, both in the Liturgy of the Word and in the eucharistic prayer, in our thanksgiving and praise and blessing of God.

One of the great blessings that the eucharist has been for Christians through the centuries is that, if we have the faith that the mystery asks of us, it brings the whole divine plan of salvation to life for us; it locates us in that plan, gives us our place there and gives us our bearings for our life's journey; it keeps fresh in our consciousness why, in God's design and by the grace of God, we exist at all; it sets our goal before us and reminds us of the numbers beyond counting who are our companions on our journey, all travelling together, helping one another, being helped by one another, as we advance; it reminds us that we follow on the path that he has taken before us and along which he is leading us.

We must nurture this awareness of faith within the eucharist and carry it over from there into our lives of every day. We identify and celebrate the divine project in the eucharist, but it is not a project confined to the eucharist; we must live it, for the rest of our lives and over the whole range of those lives, in the great and challenging and often hostile world outside the church doors.

Remember: it is God's word spoken to us with great clarity in every eucharist. Remember in faith and wonder, remember with thanksgiving and praise and blessing all that I have done for you throughout history; never forget the love and the goodness, the generosity and the abundance that it shows; remember the blessing that the gospel is, with its message of love and of salvation, with its words and commandments of life; remember that you have here the

REMEMBER AND GIVE THANKS

food you need for your journey, the food of heaven for your journey on earth, food for the mind, food for the soul, the food of life that only God can give.

And we, making all of this our own, say now to God: remember what in goodness you have done for us, remember your mercies of the past, remember your promises, remember too how frail we are, and keep faithful to it all, in spite of our fickleness, our weakness, our sin.

Remember: the word may not occur in the New Testament with the same frequency as in the Old. But so much of its power and its demand carries over from the Old into the New, as we have seen. In the early years of the Church the figure of Christ was of one living and active and ever-present, the heart of the Church's preaching and of its life. In some of those early communities there were many people who had known him and had been influenced by him and who could remember him vividly. So, the memory of Christ would have been one of the most powerful forces at work in those communities and their individual members.

And then, as time passed, the four gospels were written, all of them concerned with Christ, and concerned with him not just as a person, however influential, of the past, but as an ever-living and ever-present figure of the here and now. And there was always the eucharist, the special gift of Christ to his disciples, the means he himself chose, so that, while absent in the ordinary sense of the word, he could continue to be present to his Church, with it and in it until the end of time.

'Do this as a memorial of me,' Jesus said (Lk 22:19; 1 Cor 11:24-25): with these words he has ensured that his memory will always remain strong and vital among his followers, until he comes again.

You Gather a People to Yourself

One of the effects of the fallout from the spread of the coronavirus was our inability to gather in church as a Christian people and to celebrate the eucharist together there. For many it proved to be a very sad experience. To come together every Sunday or indeed every day for the eucharist is so much part of our Christian lives, and for many so much part of their day, that we miss it greatly while we are being deprived of it. This should not surprise us, because to gather together in Christ's name is at the heart of the very existence of the Church. The Church gathers for its eucharist because it must, because it is a law deep within it. The ecclesiastical law that requires this, important as it is, is only an outward expression of this inner law.

God Gathers the Church

This truth has its roots in the Old Testament. Again and again there we hear of God gathering the people. We should note that the initiative is God's. It was at God's command that the people came together. God it was who convoked them, through the words and actions of Moses, at Mount Sinai for the making of the covenant. It was God, through God's word, who convened them on other important occasions for the renewal of the covenant. The Jewish people were conscious of this. They recognised that God was bringing them together, so that God could be among them, to speak to them, to lead them and guide them. And it was for them to obey God's command, summons and invitation. The Old Testament speaks a lot of the people, while they wandered in the wilderness, as a congregation; it speaks too of assemblies, where they have been brought together in one way or another by God. God's people must gather as God's people, and, when they do, God is there among them.

The early Christian community had a similar sense. They recognised that they were one in Christ, but it was when they came together that they were truly the Church, the Church at some important level formed by their meeting in Christ's name and at his word. Assembly for the celebration of the eucharist in memory of Christ is in the genes of the Church from its coming into being. When persecution came, they braved even imprisonment, torture and death in faithfulness to the person of Christ within and among them, in faithfulness to what they themselves were because of that presence.

Before churches were built, they met in the house of one of their number. Thus Paul speaks twice of the church in the house of Prisca and Aquila (Rm 16:3, 5; 1 Cor 16:19), and of the church in the house of Nympha (Col 4:15).

This sense that they had is well illustrated in an account that has come down to us of the questioning of a group of Christians from Abitina in North Africa. They were apprehended while they were gathered for the *dominicum* in the house of one of their members. 'Yes, it was in my house that we were gathered for the *dominicum*,' one said. 'It is our law,' another said. 'I was there *because* I am a Christian,' said a third, and a fourth concluded his response that they were celebrating the *dominicum* because they must with the striking words: *sine dominico non possumus* (without the *dominicum* we are powerless).[11]

God Gathers an Errant People
There is a broader sense in which God gathers the people. At a time when the Jewish people were scattered in exile, God promised to

bring them together again in their homeland, in Jerusalem. The dispersal of the people was seen as more than just a fact of history. Ezekiel, for example, represents God as having scattered the people abroad, a sign of and a punishment for the inner dispersal already caused within themselves by their unfaithfulness. This is the divisive, scattering effect that sin has. But Ezekiel also spoke of God as the shepherd who will go out to search for and to rescue the lost and the strayed; and will bring the whole flock together in their own land and God will lead them and look after them there (Ez 34). God's bringing the people back from their dispersal in exile is matched by his bringing them back from the inner dispersal caused by their sins.

So too in the New Testament. Jesus portrays himself as the Good Shepherd, who looks after his sheep and keeps the flock intact. He is the shepherd who goes out to search for the lost sheep, and, when he has found it, to bring it back where it belongs. He has other sheep not yet of his flock, and these too he must gather in, because there is to be one flock and one shepherd (Jn 10:1-21).

The gospel of St John records the words of Caiaphas to members of the Sanhedrin: 'It is expedient for you that one man should die for the people,' and then the gospel adds the solemn comment: 'He did not say this of his own accord, but being high priest that year he prophesied that Jesus should die for the nation, and not for the nation only, but to gather into one the children of God who are scattered abroad' (Jn 11:49-52).

And in St John's gospel Jesus promises that when he is lifted up he will draw all people to himself – 'lifted up' (Jn 12:32): at once his being lifted up in suffering on the cross and through this his being lifted up in glory in his resurrection. In his body stretched between heaven and earth, he brings together in reconciliation God and all of humanity. In his arms outstretched horizontally, he is reaching out to all his brothers and sisters to gather them together to himself and in himself.

This theme of dispersal and gathering together is an important one in Eucharistic Prayer III. After the *Sanctus* the priest declares:

'you never cease to gather a people to yourself', words that give the title of this piece, and he does this 'so that from the rising of the sun to its setting a pure sacrifice may be offered to your name'. The prayer here is quoting words from the Old Testament, from Malachi (Mal 1:11), words that have been echoed in the Church down the centuries, right from the beginning. It is a prophecy that the Church has always seen as fulfilled in itself and in its eucharist. And if God is doing this from age to age, from east to west, from the rising of the sun to its setting, then God is doing it today, here, among those who are celebrating this eucharist.

Gathered by the Eucharist

This theme of God's gathering his people is continued explicitly through Eucharistic Prayer III. After the institution narrative and consecration, during the intercessions, it speaks of us as 'this family, whom you have summoned before you', and then it looks out over the whole world as it prays: 'In your compassion, O merciful Father, gather to yourself all your children scattered throughout the world.' This is clearly an echo of John 11:49-52, to which we have referred already, that Jesus should die 'to gather into one the children of God who are scattered abroad'.

It is especially through communion in Christ's body and blood that God achieves his purpose of gathering his people to himself. Our post-Vatican II eucharistic prayers ask at this point, in the *epiclesis*, that we who are nourished by Christ's body and blood may be filled with the Holy Spirit and become one body, one spirit in Christ (Eucharistic Prayer III). Thus, Eucharistic Prayer IV, continuing to use the language of gathering, prays that God 'grant in your loving kindness to all who partake of this one Bread and one Chalice that, gathered into one body by the Holy Spirit, they may truly become a living sacrifice in Christ to the praise of your glory'. Eucharistic Prayer II puts it more simply: 'Humbly we pray that, partaking of the Body and Blood of Christ, we may be gathered into one by the Holy Spirit.'

Communion in Christ's body and blood is communion in and with his very person; it is communion in his death and resurrection, communion in the fullness of the mystery of our salvation. That communion in Christ and with Christ is at the same time communion with one another. If we are Christ's body, then our communion with our head is also for us communion with our fellow members of the body. We who are the body of Christ receive the body of Christ in order to become all the more the body of Christ. This is God's work and must continue to be God's work. It is to be achieved in a special way in the eucharist, by the grace of Christ in us as we receive his body and blood and by the power of the Holy Spirit at work in and with and through these. The work is God's but it requires our collaboration.

God's gifts are always tasks entrusted to us too. They are given to us freely, but if we are truly to receive them and to make them our own, they can be costly too.

If we are Christ's body through the eucharist, then we must struggle to achieve that unity when we go out from the church at the end of Mass, struggling at the different levels of our community and family and personal lives.

If Christ died to gather into one the children of God scattered abroad, then that becomes our task too in whatever way we can in the world around us and in our prayers. It is all working towards God's definitive gathering of his people to himself in Christ's final coming at the end of time.

The most profound text of unity in the New Testament is Christ's great prayer at the Last Supper recorded in St John (Jn 17:1-26). As always in John, it is expressed in the simplest of language but what this expresses is truth of the deepest kind. The unity for which Christ prayed, the unity into which he and the Father work to draw his disciples, is the perfect unity that exists between the Father and himself. The effect of this is to be the witness it gives to the whole world, a witness to convince the world that Christ has indeed come from the Father, a witness to God's love made manifest in his disciples. We, the Lord's disciples, and the world as we know it are still very far from the fulfilment towards which God is calling us. This prayer of Christ's must go on unceasingly until the end of time, but Christ now joins us to himself in making his prayer.

God's work of gathering the people to himself will continue from age to age until the great final ingathering, when God will accomplish the divine plan in all its fullness. In the meantime, God expects us to engage actively and purposefully with him in striving for it. It is our task and our privilege to be God's co-workers.

eucharist ... in celebration

Word and Sacrament

We all know that Christ gave us the eucharist in the course of a meal. But we pay little attention to the fact that over the next few decades the early community began to disengage it from the meal. First, it would seem, the words and actions concerned with the bread were brought to the end of the meal, where they were joined with the words and actions concerned with the wine in a single ritual. Then this was detached altogether from the meal and to it was joined a liturgy of the word. Although the young Church remembered very clearly Christ's words, 'Do this in memory of me', it must have been convinced that it had the freedom to make this change.

As the early communities began to grow, the celebration of a meal on the occasion of the eucharist would have become more and more difficult. And we know from St Paul's first letter to the Church in Corinth (1 Cor 11:17-22) that already, about twenty-five years after the Last Supper, serious and scandalous abuse had crept into the meal there. The very meaning of the eucharist was being compromised. The Letter of Jude too refers to abuse of the community's love-feasts, and he seems to write as if this was more than a few isolated incidents (Jude 12).

The overwhelmingly Jewish make-up of the early communities meant that they would have been very familiar with the synagogue service. It was Jesus' practice, as we know, to attend the synagogue on the Sabbath and we know too that he spoke there on occasion. The Acts of the Apostles similarly recount that St Paul and his fellow missionaries preached there and gave testimony to Christ before the assembled Jews (for example, Acts 13:5, 14).

It is to be expected then that, when the early Church began to join a service of the word with its own eucharistic practice, the ritual of the synagogue should have been a strong influence. This weekly service was a liturgy of the word, with readings from scripture, preaching and prayer, and this is what the Christian liturgy of the word has been ever since.

But the bond between word and eucharist is much stronger and deeper than that.

Jesus at the Last Supper

At the Last Supper Jesus spoke at some length to the apostles. He was still preparing them for the traumatic events that were now imminent. Of the three synoptics, it is St Luke who gives us the fullest account of this and it is he who tells us about the dispute that developed among the apostles as to which of them was to be regarded as the greatest, and this after Jesus had just given them his body and blood. In his response, Jesus said that among them the first was to become as the youngest and the leader as one who serves. And he added: 'I am among you as one who serves' (Lk 22:27). Just as the gospel of St John sets the washing of the feet (Jn 13:4-16) at the point at which we might have expected an account of the institution of the eucharist, so here in St Luke we have a similar example of the humble service that is at the heart of Jesus' death and so at the heart of the eucharist as the apostles received it from him.

St John, of course, is the evangelist who gives us by far the fullest and the most profound account of Jesus' words and of his great prayer to the Father. Jesus' words at the Last Supper were a world removed from casual table-talk. He had so much that he wanted to say to his apostles – he tells them so himself (Jn 16:12) – there was so much that he knew they needed to hear. And so he spoke to them from the heart, at length and at great depth.

For our purpose here, the important thing is the context of living word provided by the Lord himself for his gift of the eucharist to his Church. And so, when the early community began to detach the eucharistic element from the meal and attach to it a more formal structure of word, this was not an extraneous addition: the word has been part of the eucharist from the beginning.

God Feeds the People

There are two texts from the Old Testament that we must consider. When the Israelites wandered for forty years, they were often exposed to great hunger and thirst. But they found that, at Moses' prayer, God cared for them in their plight; in particular, providing the bread, the daily bread, that was manna.

But they were provided for in another way too. God spoke to them on many occasions and gave them the Law to enlighten, to guide and to instruct them. It is in this context that Deuteronomy quotes Moses' words to the people: 'He humbled you and let you hunger and fed you with manna ... that he might make you know that man does not live by bread alone, but that man lives by everything that proceeds out of the mouth of the Lord' (Deut 8:3). They are words that Jesus used to effect against Satan at the end of his own time in the wilderness (Mt 4:4). God's living word too is bread for the sustenance of God's people.

Much later, this same truth will be given a somewhat different form in the Wisdom literature of the Old Testament. There, Wisdom, as God's work and with God from the beginning, is portrayed as offering a banquet, to which she invites all. Wisdom gives life, she is God's word of life, she has the food of life, she presses on all who will accept them the bread and wine of life (Prov 9:1-6; Eccles (Sir) 24:21; and, among the prophets, Bar 3:9, 13-14 and Is 55:1-3).

Jesus, God's Bread of Life

These images of the banquet of Wisdom and of God's word as bread seem to be in the background in Jesus' discourse on the bread of life in John 6. This followed closely, and indeed arose out of, Jesus' feeding the hunger of the crowd with the loaves and fish. He himself is the bread of God, which comes down from heaven and gives life to the world. Whoever comes to him in faith, accepting the claims that he makes about himself and believing his message, will never hunger or thirst. What he proclaims and teaches and preaches, what he himself lives by, is the word of God, and it is given by God to the people to be their life. In this context, Jesus reminds his hearers that it was the Father, not Moses, who gave their ancestors manna as their food in the desert, and now it is the same God who, in Jesus himself, gives the true bread of heaven to the world.

The second part of the discourse is explicitly eucharistic. Jesus' very flesh and blood will be given for the life of the world, given as the life of the world. Those who eat this bread and drink the cup abide in him and he abides in them, and they will live forever (Jn 6:54, 58). Jesus himself, both in his word and in his flesh and blood, is God's true bread given to be the life of the world.

In this discourse, it is best, I think, to see a single overarching truth; it is concerned throughout with word and eucharist together. In the first part it is the theme of the word that is explicit, but from verse 51 onwards it becomes explicitly eucharistic. But all of it tells of the bread of life, on which God feeds the hunger of the people.

Thus, it is Jesus who is the first to link word and eucharist, and he does it not in any extrinsic way but in his own person and his own life and his own words. What the Church did in the early decades was to give a more structured form to word and to eucharist and to the unity that they formed together. All of this should enhance very greatly our appreciation of the place and the status of the word in the celebration of the eucharist.

Word and Eucharist Today

One of God's great blessings to us in the Catholic Church over the last century has been the emergence of the liturgical movement and of the scriptural movement in the first half of the twentieth century. These were confirmed in due time by the encyclicals of Pope Pius XII, *Divino Afflante Spiritu* (1943) and *Mediator Dei* (1947). When the Second Vatican Council met between 1962 and 1965, the time had come, the preparatory work had largely been done, and the Council was able to give a whole new impetus to the renewal and the reform of the liturgy and to the opening of the riches of scripture to a Church ready to share in them.

In *Sacrosanctum Concilium*, the Constitution on the Liturgy, the Council decreed: 'The treasures of the Bible are to be opened up more lavishly so that a richer fare may be provided from the table of God's word ... a more representative part of the sacred scriptures will be read to the people' (51). The language of 'fare' and 'table' is worth noting here. In presenting the word as God's food given from his table to his people, the text is drawing on the much older tradition that we have been considering. Similarly, in *Dei Verbum*, the Constitution on Divine Revelation, the Council speaks of the bread of life, partaken of by the Church and offered to the faithful, as coming from the one table of the word of God and the body of Christ. This was preceded immediately by the statement: 'The Church has always venerated the divine Scriptures as she venerated the Body of the Lord.' So closely does the Council link word and eucharist that it speaks no longer of two tables but of one, the one table of word of God and body of Christ (21).

The Last Supper was unique and we cannot replicate its circumstances, but it is the same Christ who is present now both in his word and in the eucharist, present in different ways but with the single purpose of giving continuous effect to the divine mystery of salvation – a mystery already fulfilled in himself and still on the way to fulfilment in world and Church. It is this one mystery in all its fullness that is at the heart of word and sacrament: proclaimed and made present as the active, living word and the banquet of wisdom in and embodied in the living flesh of Christ, the bread of life, in the other.

In the Catholic Church for a long time we had neither a strong theology of the word nor a vibrant understanding of the part it has in the actual celebration of the eucharist. In the years since the Second Vatican Council this has been changing very quickly, to our great benefit. Words from St Jerome have been quoted many times in recent decades: 'If ... Christ is the power of God and the wisdom of God, anyone who does not know the scriptures does not know the power of God or his wisdom. Not to know the scriptures is not to know Christ.'[12] It should be noted that Jerome wrote that, not with specific reference to the New Testament, but in the prologue of his commentary on Isaiah. In other words, for Christians, Isaiah and all of the Old Testament speak of Christ. It is a truth that St Augustine too recognises when he says that the New is hidden in the Old and the Old is made manifest in the New.[13] But eminent as these writers are, there is a greater authority still. Jesus himself said to those opposing him: 'You pore over the scriptures, believing that in them you can find eternal life; it is these scriptures that testify to me' (Jn 5:39). And after his resurrection, in the company of the two disciples on the road to Emmaus, 'he interpreted to them in all the scriptures the things concerning himself' (Lk 24:27; and see 24:44). It is obvious that 'scriptures' here can refer only to the Old Testament.

Over the course of the liturgical year, the divine plan of salvation, the unfolding mystery of Christ, is recalled, but not merely as a series of past events. Word and sacrament combine to make of them events of the here and now, which actually engage us and seek our response. Christ's work of interpreting the scriptures to his followers did not end at his ascension. All through time Christ remains present among them and proclaims his word there, opening up to them the mystery of salvation, drawing them into it, and in this way continuously advancing it towards its final accomplishment.

The Lectionary of the *Roman Missal*

It is not my purpose to treat of the Lectionary here, but a few comments are in order.

All will have their disagreement about the choice or the omission of this or that text. There will be questions too about the editing of individual pericopes. There are those who have reservations about the decision to link the choice of Old Testament readings to the gospel on the Sundays of Ordinary Time or about the particular reading chosen.

But all must acknowledge what the compilers brought to their work and what they achieved there for the Church: the breadth and the seriousness of the purpose they set before themselves in their effort to execute faithfully the Council's decree; the depth of understanding of the centrality of the word of God in the Church's life and especially in the celebration of the eucharist; the principles and structures that they developed in pursuing their purpose.

Those who remember the extremely limited selection of readings in the pre-Vatican II *Roman Missal* know that they have special reason to be grateful for the decree of *Sacrosanctum Concilium,* the Constitution on the Liturgy, and for the Lectionary that emerged in response to it. We recognise the human contribution, but, as in everything that touches the scriptures, we must recognise the work of the Holy Spirit, underpinning and directing and giving life to it all. For this we give thanks to God.

10

Body and Blood

We are so familiar with Christ's words 'body and blood' or 'flesh and blood' and with the pair closely associated with them, 'bread and wine', that we fail to see what a surprising choice of words it was. While in the accounts we have of the Last Supper Jesus speaks of his 'body' and 'blood', in his discourse on the bread of life in John 6 he uses 'flesh' consistently throughout in place of 'body'. This suggests that for our purpose here the two are to be taken as synonyms.

If Jesus wanted a means by which he could be present in his Church until the end of time, why choose things as fragile and as transient as bread and wine? In his place, if we wanted to be remembered for generations to come, we would surely choose something that we would regard as more worthy, more impressive, something solid and abiding to stand the test of time. But Christ chose bread and wine to be the outward sign of his enduring presence. And why use the words 'body and blood' or 'flesh and blood' to speak of himself present in this way? There is nothing obvious in this. What is he teaching us here?

At another time and in a different context, Christ used the expression 'flesh and blood'. It was when Peter made his profession that Jesus was 'the Christ, the Son of the living God' (Mt 16:16). Jesus responded by saying that it was not 'flesh and blood' that had revealed this to him but Jesus' own Father in heaven (Mt 16:17). Here 'flesh and blood' obviously stands for a human being, with the suggestion of human limitation and weakness – much as we still use the phrase today. And in a similar sense St Paul tells the Galatians that when God revealed Christ to him in order to preach him among the Gentiles, he did not confer with flesh and blood, not with those who were apostles before him, but went into Arabia and then back to Damascus (Gal 1:15-17). Again, St Paul is emphasising very strongly God's action in his life, and what he owes to God, and this he contrasts with what human beings might have done for him.

But Jesus, at the Last Supper and in the discourse of John 6, intended something a lot richer and deeper than this important, though general, sense conveys.

To a Jew of that time, 'flesh and blood' or 'body and blood' would have called up images of sacrifice. Simply in his choice of these words in this context, there is already a pointer to a sacrificial understanding and intent on Jesus' part. This might have been less immediately obvious to his apostles at the Last Supper itself, where, according to St Paul (1 Cor 11:23-25) and St Luke (Lk 22:19-20), Jesus' words over the bread and his words over the wine were separated by the meal they were sharing. This changed quickly; the two sets of words and of actions were joined together, they became detached from the meal, and from this emerged the eucharist in the form in which the Church has celebrated it ever since. With this, Jesus' words over the bread and over the wine were set down side by side, and this relationship helped the Church to understand 'body' and 'blood' in a deeper way.

In addition, there was the context of the paschal meal. The body of the paschal lamb was to be sacrificed and then roasted and eaten. The blood of the lamb had been sprinkled on the doors and the lintels of each house on that first night, and in that way had served to save those living there from God's destroying angel.

The three synoptics identify the Last Supper as a paschal meal, while St John places Jesus' death at just the hour at which the paschal lamb was being sacrificed in the Temple. And immediately after

Christ's death, while his body still hung on the cross, John makes his understanding very clear: Christ himself is the paschal lamb. In John's chronology the meal would have been taken only after Jesus' death.

Were there two calendars in use? Or did Jesus celebrate the paschal meal in his own way and at a time of his own choosing? For our purpose here, we do not have to provide an answer. The paschal references and the paschal context are deliberate and point towards a paschal intention on Christ's part and a paschal interpretation of the event on the part of all four evangelists. St Paul's account (1 Cor 11:23-27) does not help us in this regard, but in the same letter he too makes an explicit paschal reference: 'Christ, our paschal lamb, has been sacrificed' (1 Cor 5:7).

The Accounts of Institution

Scripture has four accounts of the institution of the eucharist: from Paul (1 Cor 11:23-27) and from the three synoptics. Of these, Mark and Matthew are very close and form a pair; so too Paul and Luke. St Paul's is the oldest written account we have – written about twenty-five years after the actual event. But he reminds the church in Corinth that what he passed on to them was what he himself had received from the Lord. This then would take us back to the time of his conversion or very shortly after. This means that his account was already being passed down in the community just a couple of years after the Last Supper itself. This gives us strong reassurance of its reliability.

Similarly in the case of the synoptics. Their accounts would have been circulating in the community, probably in the actual celebration of the eucharist in different localities, long before they were written down in the gospels.

St John, as we know, has no account of the institution of the eucharist in his chapters about the Last Supper. At the point at which we might have expected it, he tells us instead of the washing of the feet, an event that brings out graphically something of the deeper meaning of the celebration of the eucharist as Jesus intended it: humble, mutual service and support of one another. Earlier, of course, in chapter six, he had presented Jesus' great discourse on the bread of life. One line there calls for comment in this context: 'The bread that I shall give is my flesh for the life of the world' (Jn 6:51). Substitute 'body' for 'flesh', and this sentence then bears a strong resemblance to Jesus' own words over the bread as we find them in Paul and Luke.

But Christ said more than 'This is my body ... This is my blood', and the words he used help us to enter more deeply into his understanding of his approaching death and of the divine purpose that he recognised there.

Mark and Matthew record Jesus as saying over the bread: 'This is my body' (Mk 14:22; Mt 26:26). While Paul adds after 'body' 'which is for you' (1 Cor 11:24) and Luke has 'which is given for you' (Lk 22:19). In the context of the Last Supper and of the whole account of what Jesus said there, this must be taken as a reference to his impending death. Jesus' death is offered for the disciples; it is a sacrifice that he is making of himself for them. He is interpreting his death for them, and in his words and actions at the Last Supper he is anticipating it.

An examination of his words over the cup leads to the same conclusion and carries us even more deeply into the mystery of his death. Both Mark and Matthew have: 'This is my blood of the covenant, which is poured out for many' (Mk 14:24; Mt 26:28). While Matthew adds to it: 'for the forgiveness of sins' (Mt 26:28). Paul's account reads: 'This cup is the new covenant in my blood' (1 Cor 11:25). While Luke has: 'This cup which is poured out is the new covenant in my blood' (Lk 22:20). All four link Jesus' death to the blood of the covenant: Paul and Luke speak of 'new covenant' (1 Cor 11:24; Lk 22:20).

This immediately calls to mind the scene in Exodus 24, in which the covenant was made between God and God's people on Mount Sinai. Israel offered sacrifice to God, and then Moses took some of the blood and threw it upon the people, saying: 'Behold the blood of the covenant which the Lord has made with you' (Ex 24:8). The echo of this text in Christ's words is unmistakable. He is offering his life in sacrifice and the blood of that sacrifice seals the covenant, but this time it is a new covenant that God is inaugurating with the people.

The great text that speaks of the new covenant is Jeremiah 31:31-34: 'Behold the days are coming, says the Lord, when I will make a new covenant with the house of Israel and the house of Judah.' This will not be like the earlier covenant, which they broke. In this new covenant the law of God will be written on the hearts; God will be their God and they will be God's people; all will know God as their God, who will forgive their iniquity and remember their sin no more. The new covenant then will bring with it God's forgiveness, and in Matthew's account Jesus makes this explicit when he adds: 'for the forgiveness of sins' (Mt 26:28).

There is one other set of texts from the Old Testament to which Jesus seems to allude in the words he spoke. The fourth Song of the Servant in Isaiah portrays the servant as bearing our griefs and carrying our sorrows, wounded for our transgressions, bruised for our iniquities, one on whom the Lord has laid the iniquity of us all, one who makes of himself an offering for sin (Is 53:4-6,10). There is a striking general parallel here between Jesus as he goes to his death and God's Servant as presented in this passage. There are notable verbal echoes as well. The Servant will make 'many to be accounted righteous' (11), he 'bore the sin of many', he 'poured out his soul to death' (12). There are good grounds for saying that when Jesus says of his body 'which is (given) for you', when he speaks of his blood 'poured out for you' or 'poured out for many', he is pointing to the Servant portrayed in Isaiah and is in fact identifying himself with this mysterious figure. There is some further support for this in the words of Jesus that only Matthew records: 'poured out ... for the forgiveness of sins' (Mt 26:28). We recall too that earlier in his ministry Jesus said the Son of Man came not to be served but to serve and to give his life as a ransom for many (Mt 20:28; Mk 10:45). Again, Jesus seems to apply to himself what Isaiah prophesied about the Servant and to identify himself with the Servant.

The few actions and words of Jesus that the scriptural accounts have passed on to us are very rich in themselves and in the understanding that they open up to us of what Jesus himself thought and intended as he sat at table on that last night and looked ahead to what he was to do the next day.

Take and Eat, Take and Drink

All of this may seem far removed from our experience, remote in time, remote in language, remote even to a degree in understanding. But what brings its reality very close to us, and catches us up into it, is what Jesus said to his apostles at the Last Supper and what he says to us since then in every celebration of the eucharist: 'Take and eat ... Take and drink.' Collectively and individually, they and we are to enter the mystery of Christ's death in all its fullness by eating his body and drinking his blood; we are to be brought by him into the sacrificial offering that he is making of himself, the sacrificial offering by which Christ will bring in the promised new covenant and seal it solemnly and forever.

When we do in the Lord's memory what we have been bidden to do, when we eat his body and drink his blood, we are joined in communion through him to the one who declares himself to be our God. Every time we celebrate the eucharist, we are given once again his commitment of himself to his people and to us who are gathered here today in his presence. And we for our part commit ourselves to what the covenant asks of us. In this way, the new covenant is not just an event of two thousand years ago at which we were not present. It is a reality for us here and now, a reality of every Sunday and indeed of every day, wherever Christ's disciples come together to celebrate the eucharist.

Christ chose elements of a meal to serve his purpose; he adapted himself to the nature of bread and of wine. These together suggest the one meal, but in their individuality each makes its own distinctive contribution to that one meal. In the eucharist Christ uses this to draw us by distinct, though intimately related, ways into the one mystery of his life and death, and of its fruits for us.

Body, Blood

When Christ speaks of his body and blood here, what is he referring to? Is it his body somehow separated from his blood, his blood somehow separated from his body? This cannot be so. A mediaeval doctrine invoked in answer always insisted that where Christ's body is present, there too by concomitance are his blood, soul and divinity, and where Christ's blood is present, there too by concomitance are his body, soul and divinity.

We can express this same truth today in a different way. Body and blood are not to be taken disjunctively but together. Together they refer to Christ in all the fullness of his being. In the Old Testament, blood was the carrier of life. And so, this is no mere appearance or sign of Christ, no mere spiritual or virtual presence. This is the whole Christ present in all the hard reality of his embodied self; this is the whole Christ present in his very life-blood – the whole Christ present in the totality of his living being. It is the one Christ, fully present in both his body and blood, but by speaking as he did, distinguishing his body and his blood, he invites us to see the fullness of his mystery under different lights and so to advance more deeply in our understanding and in our participation in it.

Why Bread and Wine?

Back to a question raised at the start. Why did our Lord choose such common and such perishable elements as bread and wine to be the means of his enduring presence? I am sure that there can be many attempts at explanation, but here I offer only one.

The answer must be intimately related to ourselves, since it was for us and for our salvation that Christ came on earth in the first place. Now, towards the end of his life, he desires to remain present on earth even after the ascension, continuously with his people in a special way all through history, continuously working among them to realise the great plan of God. How best would he accomplish that? It was with this in mind that he made his choice, the choice that would be best suited to us in our world, to our nature and our need.

It is a choice that we in our little knowledge or wisdom would never have imagined.

It is a form of presence that is fragile, one might think unworthy; it is a form that will endure and yet is always passing and must be renewed every Sunday and every day. We are very familiar with the human reality of our daily meals, a necessary and permanent reality of our lives and yet one that is transient and must be renewed from one day to the next. We recognise our fundamental need of food and drink for our continued well-being and even existence.

Christ was surely tapping into that in his choice of bread and wine for his great purpose. But our food and drink should never be taken for granted. That is why we have the tradition, inherited from Old Testament times, of saying grace before and after meals. Food and drink are ultimately gifts of God and they have to be worked for continually; they have to be provided for us by others and by our own effort. Whenever we receive them, we acknowledge this fact before God.

Similarly, Christ's presence is never to be taken for granted. As Church and as individuals we need that presence, and it comes to us as a gift in every eucharist. It is a gift to be recognised for what it is, a gift to be prayed for humbly but confidently, a gift always to be received with thanksgiving.

Christ's presence to us in our eucharistic food and drink is far more intimate than any form of presence in a permanent object or structure could ever be. It makes it possible for him to become part of us and it allows us to become part of him in a uniquely personal way and at a depth that such external forms could never do. It works to achieve its purpose not just from outside but from deep within, and it can evoke a response from us, a response of engagement, a response of our whole life and being, a response of love. And this work of Christ in the eucharist is unending, renewed every Sunday and every day of the week to draw from us a response that will be lifelong because it is being constantly renewed.

11

The Mystery of Faith

Some older readers will remember a time when the phrase 'the mystery of faith' was used in every Mass, placed in the middle of Jesus' words over the chalice at the Last Supper. At some point it had been inserted into the Roman Canon (now also called Eucharistic Prayer I), and there it remained for many centuries: 'This is the chalice of my blood, the blood of the new and eternal covenant, the mystery of faith, which will be poured out for you and for many for the forgiveness of sins.' In the renewal and reform of the eucharist after the Second Vatican Council, the phrase was removed and placed immediately after the institution narrative and consecration, a place at which in a number of Eastern liturgies there is indeed an acclamation of Christ.

What do these words mean and what part do they play in the unfolding of the eucharistic mystery?

The phrase itself occurs for the first time in the first letter to Timothy: 'Great is the mystery of our faith. He was made visible in the flesh, justified in the Spirit, seen by angels, proclaimed to the gentiles, believed in throughout the world, taken up in glory' (1 Tm 3:16). The first thing to note is that the word 'mystery' used here by Paul refers to Christ. Christ himself is the mystery of faith: Christ over the whole range of his life, Christ in his paschal mystery. Paul here may well be quoting a still older acclamation of Christ that was already in circulation in the early community. Its ancient roots, its use by Paul, its place for many centuries at the very heart of the Mass make it a word of great depth and richness and weight for us.

The thinking of St Paul is clearly evident elsewhere when Christ is spoken of as the 'mystery', the secret plan of God, kept hidden from the beginning but now in God's good time revealed by him in Christ, revealed not just in his words but in the total event of his life, death and resurrection (Col 1:26, 27, 2:2, 4:3; Eph 1:9, 3:3-6, 9, 5:32). And it is not merely that he reveals the secret of the divine plan. The plan is embodied in him and implemented in a decisive way in him. He is its very centre point around which everything turns. This is the Christ who is the mystery of faith.

When the words 'mystery of faith' were inserted into Jesus' words over the chalice the context confirmed how they were to be understood there. The mystery of faith is Christ's blood, and in that blood Christ himself, given in sacrifice to the Father, the blood that thereby inaugurated the new and eternal covenant and brings the forgiveness of sins. This is fully consistent with what we have seen of their use in the thinking of St Paul.

Later, 'the mystery of faith' will come to be understood in a narrower sense, as referring to the true presence of Christ in his body and his blood, what for long we called 'the real presence'.

In the light of this, it is instructive to look at the phrase in the Mass as revised after the Second Vatican Council. It is now placed after the institution narrative and consecration as an invitation seeking a response, and the response is made to Christ. The three forms of acclamation given agree in their content: the mystery of faith is Christ in his paschal mystery. None of the three spells out all the moments of this, but taken together they speak of Christ's death, resurrection and second coming. What is perhaps a little unexpected here is the reference to the second coming. But it is to be found already in Paul: 'Wherever you eat this bread and drink the cup, you are proclaiming his death until he comes' (1 Cor 11:26), and of course this text has been adapted slightly to give us what is now the second form of our response.

When Paul says, 'until he comes', he is not using the phrase exclusively or even primarily in its chronological reference, as if to say that we will go on celebrating the eucharist through the centuries until eventually the Lord will come. He means that the second coming is already in some way anticipated, even present, in Christ's death and resurrection, and this is part of what we celebrate each time we gather for the eucharist. The chronological reference is there too, of course, and taken together these give a content of great richness to his words.

There is confirmation of this in a number of Eastern liturgies. There, in the *anamnesis*, the memorial prayer that follows immediately on the acclamation, as it does in the Roman Rite, we make memorial of Christ's death, his resurrection, his ascension – and his second coming. As presented there, it is something that we are said to remember, something that in some sense must be already pre-contained in his great paschal mystery as part of that mystery. It is an important statement of the eschatological dimension of what we celebrate in the Mass.

All of this is the mystery of faith that is at the heart of the eucharist.

My Lord and My God

Again, older readers will recall that during the elevation of the host and the elevation of the chalice, we were encouraged to say, with St Thomas: 'My Lord and my God' (Jn 20:28). It is said that Cardinal William Conway obtained approval from Rome for the inclusion of this as an additional response in the missal for Ireland, on the grounds that it was a phrase already well known and loved in this context by the Irish Church. And so, it was included in the missal published jointly in England and Wales, Scotland, Ireland under the rubric 'in Ireland only'. Its difference from the other three versions of the response is marked, especially when account is taken of its previous use as an acclamation of Christ's real presence under the forms of bread and wine.

However, of itself it does not have to be understood as an acknowledgement of faith in Christ's presence in the eucharist. This is not the context in which St Thomas used it originally, according to St John's gospel (Jn 20:28), and that context is important. Thomas was one of Jesus' closest disciples. The twelve apostles had been chosen by Jesus himself and had been with him from the early days. They had come to accept him as one specially sent by God, they had believed his teaching and had stayed faithfully with him right up to his arrest and passion. When he came among them on the evening of that first, great Sunday, they accepted that he had indeed risen from the dead. But not Thomas. He remained stubborn in his refusal to believe. And that is the context in which, in response to Jesus' invitation to believe, he made his great profession: 'My Lord and my God.'

Among Jews 'Lord' was very commonly used as a substitute for the divine name. But up to this point no one in the gospels had said this of Jesus. Thomas accepted now that Jesus had indeed risen from the dead, but he took a huge step further in acclaiming him as his Lord and God. This Jesus whom they had accepted and followed, this Jesus who had suffered his passion and his ignominious death, this Jesus whom they had abandoned in his hour of greatest need, this Jesus who had risen from the dead – this Jesus is now recognised for the first time as Lord and God. It took the experience of his life and death and resurrection before even his closest friends could recognise him for what he truly is and acclaim him Lord and God. If we use Thomas' words in the eucharist, it is in this context of the paschal mystery in all its fullness that we should understand them.

The Eucharist and the Creed
On Sundays and solemnities we say the Creed in the profession of our faith. In the early Church, in the preparation for adult baptism, the public proclamation of the Creed by the catechumens had an important place. And right down to the present, in infant baptism,

the public declaration of the faith by the parents and godparents has been very closely tied to the moment of baptism itself. Baptism in particular is the sacrament of faith. And so, in our practice of reciting the Creed during Mass on Sundays and major feasts, there is an echo of baptism and a reminder that the eucharist, among many things, is a renewal of baptism and has been so from the beginning.

This recital of the Creed in common during Mass is not, as it were, the addition of an extraneous element to the Mass. It is more like the explicit declaration of a reality that is already there, deeply embedded in the nature of the eucharist itself but here brought to the surface and acknowledged. We could say that the eucharist is the Creed in prayer form.

This is true of the Mass in its entirety, but it can be seen in a more precise way if we set the Apostles' Creed and Eucharistic Prayer IV (or a number of the great corresponding anaphoras of the Eastern Church) in parallel. All of the mysteries of the Creed are there, but expressed in a fuller way. Thus, the opening lines of Eucharistic Prayer IV can be seen to be an expansion in thanksgiving and praise and glorification of the doctrine of God the Creator. The central section of both is concerned with Christ, his incarnation, the paschal mystery of his death, resurrection and ascension, and the evocation of his second coming, as we have seen earlier. The Creed goes on to mention briefly the Holy Spirit, while the eucharistic prayer speaks of his role in the world and in particular in the eucharist. The holy Catholic Church and the communion of saints feature strongly in the intercessions of the eucharistic prayer, while the prayers for the dead there are based on belief in the resurrection of the body and life everlasting. The doctrine of the forgiveness of sins underlines much of the prayer and is mentioned explicitly in our Lord's words over the chalice.

All of this may appear schematic and artificial, but it does illustrate the unbreakable bond that there is between faith and the Church's liturgy. The eucharist is indeed our faith expressed as prayer and in prayer.

What does all this say to us? Surely that the eucharist is not just a devotional prayer, that its very foundation is the truth proclaimed and lived out by Christ and made its own by the Church in its Creed; that it is the identical truth that both Creed and eucharist profess in their different ways; that in the eucharist the great mysteries of the Church's faith are, as it were, engaged and brought to life for us, the members of the Church; that word and sacrament are most intimately connected in the preaching and the life of the Church. The eucharist is indeed the mystery of faith *par excellence.*

12

Preparing for Communion

The Our Father is a prayer for every occasion, but it is nowhere more at home than in the sacrament of baptism and in the Mass. Its place in baptism is obvious. It is there that we are united with Christ, the Son of God, as his brothers and sisters, it is there that, in Christ, the Father adopts us as his sons and daughters and introduces us into his family – and all of this by the working on us and in us of the Holy Spirit, the bond of unity and of love within the Trinity.

It is the place of the Lord's Prayer in the eucharist, to begin with, that concerns me here.

In the early Church there was a very strong awareness that the eucharist was the sacramental climax of Christian initiation. Not long before their baptism, the catechumens were formally introduced to the Our Father and given its wording. They were to make the prayer their own in anticipation of their praying it with the whole Christian family at their initiation. Their baptism was carried out apart; then they were brought into the assembly of their new sisters and brothers and they joined with them in celebrating the eucharist and saying with them for the first time the Our Father. There is a similar pattern to the Order of Christian Initiation of Adults (RCIA), restored to the Church in the wake of the Second Vatican Council after a long absence.

In the light of this we can see that every eucharist is in an important way a renewal of our baptism, a celebration of the fact that, because of it, all of us together are the family of God and each of us is a daughter or son of the Father.

And so, when we join our hearts and our voices in saying or singing the Our Father, it is not just any prayer that we are making. This is a re-affirmation in faith of what God has made us, together and individually; it is the prayer *par excellence* that gives voice to what we are in the depth of our being. It is the prayer given to us by the Lord himself, in whom and with whom we rejoice in our status as children of the Father. Although neither Christ nor the Holy Spirit is mentioned in it, it is a prayer that we can make only in union with Christ and by the working within us of the Spirit.

It is a prayer that we make always in the communion of our brothers and sisters. As is clear from its opening word, and however isolated we may feel on the occasion as we say it, we never stand alone before God.

The Place of the Lord's Prayer

From an early stage there was agreement in the Church, East and West, that the Our Father be included in the eucharist, and agreement too about its place: just before the distribution of communion. This is where it was in the Roman Rite in the early centuries. But Pope Gregory the Great (590–604), in the face of some opposition, moved it to the position it has occupied ever since, at the very beginning of the rite of communion. It was a decision that has justified itself over the centuries.

Placed where it is, it makes a smooth transition from the eucharistic prayer to what follows. The eucharistic prayer is spoken by the priest both in the name of Christ and in the name of the whole assembly. It is made through, with and in Christ in the unity of the Holy Spirit, as the final doxology expressly states. The Our Father, in its address and in its first three petitions with their focus on God, can be thought to look back in a sense to the eucharistic prayer and prolong it briefly, while at the same time moving us gently on to the petitions that look forward to the act of communion. Two of these are particularly appropriate at this point: 'Give us this day our daily bread, and forgive us our trespasses, as we forgive those who trespass against us.'

Though in themselves wider in scope, in this context these are to be given a eucharistic interpretation. Standing at the beginning is the prayer that will inform all that follows: 'Give us this day our daily bread,' here understood as the body of Christ. It is followed by the prayer for forgiveness, God's forgiveness of us, our forgiveness of one another. This is the condition on which God will make us ready to receive this daily bread. The two petitions will be repeated and developed right up to the act of communion.

Peace, Forgiveness
In passing on to this, we note the easy movement from the Our Father into the prayer that follows: 'deliver us from evil … Deliver us, Lord, from every evil …' Deliver us from the all-pervasive reality of sin in the world, from its power, from its source, the evil one; and deliver us from all the particular forms and manifestations of this evil. And then this is extended into a petition for peace and for freedom from sin and deliverance from all distress.

Peace here is not just the absence of war and strife and turmoil, not just inner or outward tranquillity. It is also, and especially, the peace of which Christ spoke at the Last Supper (Jn 14:27), the peace that only he can give, the peace of sins forgiven, the peace of being at one with God. This is made explicit in the following prayer and leads into the sign of peace. We cannot be at peace with God if we are not at peace with one another, as Our Lord insisted in the petition of the Our Father. Indeed, as we can see, he made it a condition and a measure of the divine forgiveness that we seek for ourselves. These themes are larger than we have been portraying them, but in the communion rite of the Mass they have a special relevance and are particularly apposite.

The Our Father is admirably suited to be used as a communion prayer, placed with great insight by Gregory the Great to open the communion rite and to set the agenda for what follows, in order that as a people and individually we may receive worthily from God our daily bread.

Our Daily Bread

At this point it is appropriate to turn to a question debated by scholars. 'Our daily bread' is an expression that has long been part of our ordinary vocabulary. It is simple and familiar, homely even, and we have a clear understanding of what we mean by it. But there are scholars who query if this is precisely what Jesus meant. They point out that the Greek word in the scriptural accounts is an unusual one and is open to other interpretations. Does it actually mean 'tomorrow's bread', the bread of the world to come? This sounds very strange to our ears, but we should not dismiss it out of hand. The bread of the eucharist is indeed tomorrow's bread given us today as a promise in anticipation by God. It is the bread that is an earnest of the food of heaven; even now it gives a foretaste of the life that awaits us in heaven. Our long tradition has always recognised this, and indeed it is already there in Our Lord's discourse on the bread of life.

Still another possible translation of the original Greek is 'supersubstantial' and this has the support of an early Latin translation of the scriptures. This means that it has been raised to a level higher than what makes it what it is in the natural order. Once again, we have a long and a strong tradition that the bread of the eucharist is indeed supersubstantial.

We will continue, of course, to use 'daily bread' and this is how we will continue to say the Lord's Prayer. But we should not exclude from our minds these other possible meanings. Some will be surprised, dismayed even, to think that there could be disagreement about what Jesus meant by these words from the prayer he taught us, words that have won a special place at the heart of our prayer. But instead of seeing as confusing what is simple, clear and traditional, should we not rather see in it an enrichment that enhances and expands our understanding, that opens up for us unexpected levels of fullness that are there, as so often they are, in Jesus' words? Christ's body is indeed our daily bread; it is supersubstantial bread too, and it is tomorrow's bread, the food of the world to come. This mysterious and wonderful bread is what we seek from God for today.

The Supper of the Lamb

There is a hint, and more than a hint, of tomorrow's bread in the words said by the priest as he holds up the host for all to see: 'Behold the Lamb of God ...' The second sentence goes on: 'Blessed are those called to the supper of the Lamb.' These words were added in the revision of the Missal following the Second Vatican Council. For a time, shortly after they were introduced, a number of priests used to say, in the version of the time: 'Happy are *we* who are called to his supper.' It was an attempt to make the words and the act of communion more personal for the people present.

But it was mistaken. There is an important scriptural reference here, which they did not recognise and indeed which that translation did not help them to recognise. The words are a straight quotation from Apocalypse 19:9. There they refer to the wedding feast in heaven of the Lamb and his bride, the Church. But the scene as presented in the Apocalypse is also open to the interpretation that in some way this is already beginning even now.

We can distinguish three levels here: blessed are those (and so, we among them) who are called to receive the Lord's body whenever we share in the eucharist; blessed are those who, in sharing the bread of God here and now, are thereby given a promise of sharing that bread in the world to come; blessed are those who in the final consummation will be called to the great wedding feast of heaven. We can distinguish these levels but we should not separate them.

But there is a warning here too. To be invited to share at the first two of these levels is no guarantee of an invitation at the third, final level. There is a long road and a lot of preparation before us at the first two if the Lord is to find us fit to be called at the third.

And even at the first two levels, none of us present can take it for granted that the Lord is calling us. We must be fit on every occasion to receive his call. St Paul knew that, as he shows in his words of severe condemnation of the Corinthians for their conduct at what he calls the Lord's Supper (1 Cor 11:20). And one of the prayers of the priest in preparation for communion asks: 'Let it not bring me to judgement and condemnation.' If for a long time in the past people received the eucharist very infrequently out of a strong sense of reverence or even fear, it is a warning that we in the present need to hear and to take to heart. And it is a prayer that all of us need to make, with great humility.

Placed as it is between the high points of the eucharistic prayer and our partaking of Christ's body and blood, this part of the communion rite does not always get from us the attention or the concentration that it merits. But this part of the Mass has a lot to say to us about communion itself and about what it demands of us in preparation, as God's family and as individual members of this family. And not just to say to us but to offer help and support in making us ready to receive the Lord when he comes to us in his sacrament and in making us ready to be received by him when he calls us to his marriage feast.

13

The Lamb of God

I had completed this piece when a basic and obvious question struck me for the first time. Lamb of God: what is the relationship between the Lamb and God here? In other words, what does 'of' stand for here? Does it mean that the lamb belongs to God and comes from him for his purpose? Or does it mean that the lamb comes from us but now belongs to God because it has been made over to him, offered to him in sacrifice? Or is the 'of' simply epexegetical, the Lamb who is God, as we might say 'the City of Derry', or the 'County of Armagh', or 'the Hill of Tara', or 'the Island of Ireland', when we mean the City that is Derry, the County that is Armagh, the Hill that is Tara, the Island that is Ireland? For the present, it is enough just to have raised the question.

We know the words well from their place in the eucharist just before communion; every time we are at Mass, as member of the congregation or as minister or as priest, we use them. But, once again, because of that familiarity we may close ourselves to the rich content that they have.

According to the gospel of St John, they were first applied to Jesus by John the Baptist, who used them to identify Jesus very early on, when he was just beginning his public life (Jn 1:35). It is a designation of great fullness and depth because of its place in two important passages of the Old Testament.

The first is in the events leading up to the Exodus, where the people, enslaved in Egypt, were commanded by God to take a lamb, to slay it and to sprinkle its blood on the lintels of the houses where they were staying. Later that night, when the angel of the Lord went through Egypt slaying all the first-born of the land, on seeing the blood he spared or 'passed over' the houses on which it had been sprinkled. So significant was this event for the Jewish people, that, again at God's command, they observed the annual memorial of this event in a solemn ritual (Ex 12:1-28). The paschal lambs were slain in the Temple in the afternoon and eaten at the paschal meal at home in the evening, when people gathered as family units. Thus, in calling Jesus the Lamb of God, St John would have been identifying Jesus as the paschal lamb right from the beginning of his public life.

This conclusion is strengthened by the fact that in John's chronology the Last Supper was not the paschal meal. This would be celebrated the following evening. What this meant was that Jesus was put to death at just the hour that the paschal lambs were being slaughtered in the Temple. In John's gospel this is not just an interesting coincidence. When the Roman soldiers saw that Jesus had died on the cross, they did not break his legs, as had been their intention, but pierced his side with a lance. John adds the comment that this was in fulfilment of a text 'you shall not break a bone of him' (Jn 19:36; see Ps 34 (33):21, Ex 12:46). The significance of this is that it is taken from the prescriptions about the paschal lamb. Again, this is not fortuitous. John is identifying Jesus as the paschal lamb, slain for the salvation of his people. Thus, in John's gospel, Jesus is identified as the Lamb of God right from the beginning of his public life, and now, at the end, his identity is confirmed: he is indeed the Lamb of God, who in dying has completed the mission given to him, who has taken on himself the sins of the world and died for the salvation of his people.

The title 'Lamb of God' may also have a reference to the sacrificial lamb of the fourth of the Songs of the Servant in Isaiah 53 (Is 52:13–53:12). Like a lamb, he was led to the slaughter, carrying our sins and transgressions, and by his wounds we are healed. Isaiah develops the theme through this memorable and moving chapter. To whom he was referring originally is not clear, but these are songs that Jesus seems to have taken to himself. He seems to be echoing them in some of his sayings, not least at the Last Supper when he speaks of his blood poured out 'for many' (Mk 14:24), an idea and a phrase prominent in Isaiah's prophecy.

Scholars will have their discussions about the finer points of this, but the overall truth will remain. It is of interest to note that for long the Song of the Servant in Isaiah 53 and the Passion according to the gospel of St John have been read together in our liturgy on Good Friday.

So much for the pre-history of the title, for its application to Christ and its fulfilment in him in his death.

The Lamb of God

But then in the Apocalypse the title is taken up again and used of Christ in glory. The Lamb of God is a dominant figure of the Apocalypse. His work on earth has been completed but it remains in him in glory as a very powerful and living reality. It has made him what he will be forever: the Lamb that was slain. And the effects of his redemptive death live on too in the multitude that continue to look to him in heaven and continue to follow him and to acknowledge all that they owe to him. The deliberate emphasis throughout on the sacrificial character of the Lamb's death harks back to John the Baptist's simple reference to the Lamb of God in John 1:35 and to the background of the title in the Old Testament, as we have considered it earlier. This is no passing theme of the Apocalypse; it recurs all through the book and is worked in and through the message that the author gives there. 'Lamb of God' is not just a title of honour then but a true identification of who this glorified Christ is and what he has become and what he has achieved through the life he lived and the death he died.

Now he is seated with God in the glory of heaven, receiving all the worship and blessing and praise and glory of those whom he has saved, those who have been washed clean in his blood. And not just of this human creation. Together with the One seated on the throne, he is worshipped too by countless numbers of angels, the great court of heaven. 'Then I heard all the living things in creation, everything that lives in heaven, and on earth, and under the earth, and in the sea, crying: "To the One seated on the throne and to the Lamb be all praise, honour, glory and power, for ever and ever"' (Apoc 5:13). Not only does he receive the worship of all creation, together with the One seated on the throne, but the text suggests that he leads the victorious in the great song in praise of the Lord God Almighty, what the text calls: 'the hymn of the Lamb.'

But his is not otherwise a largely passive existence in heaven. The Lamb alone has the power to take the scroll, to break open its seals, and to reveal the mysteries yet to come. He will continue to be the shepherd of God's people and in their need will protect them and guide them to springs of living water (Apoc 7:17). With his faithful followers he will defeat the powers of evil (Apoc 17:14).

The final chapters of the Apocalypse look to the consummation of all things in the final and definitive reign of God. It is presented as the wedding feast of the Lamb and of his radiant bride. 'Blessed are those who are called to the wedding feast of the Lamb' (19:9), words familiar to us from the communion rite of the Mass and that I have alluded to earlier in the previous chapter, words that, occurring where they do in the Mass, bring us here in the present very close to that final, God-willed fulfilment of the great divine project in the glory of heaven.

The radiant bride is the new Jerusalem, God's holy city. There is no temple in this city since the Lord God Almighty and the Lamb are themselves the temple, just as they are the light that illumines it. From the throne of God and of the Lamb, too, rises the river of life.

A simple title in the first chapter of John's gospel has been expanded here in the Apocalypse into a very profound presentation of what the life and death of the Lamb have achieved for multitudes up to the present and of what they will continue to achieve for the multitudes still to come. 'Lamb of God' is not just an unusual title used once, at the beginning of Christ's public ministry. It is a title that can be understood to convey his whole life here on earth, issuing in his sacrificial death on the cross, and then summing up his whole heavenly existence and activity. In that simple title we have a rich, complex, coherent statement of the whole event or mystery of Christ in itself and in what it achieved and will go on achieving for all creation. The Apocalypse is a difficult and often obscure book but in its presentation of the Lamb that was slain and now shares the throne of God, it opens up to us in a new way so much of our traditional doctrine of Christ's redemptive work for us and the great promise that awaits us, the luminous hope that it gives.

Innocent Suffering

It is of interest to many people seeking to have a fuller understanding of the eucharist to go behind its prayers and phrases in order to find more of the riches and of the depths that are there. It should help them in the understanding they bring to their participation in the eucharist and so enhance their appreciation of the mystery. But can we go a little further, to see not just an effect on the mind but on the heart too and on the life we live?

The Lamb is an image of innocence and the slaughter of the lamb a very telling and moving image of innocent suffering. The picture of Christ exposed to his passion and suspended in agony on the cross is so powerful that perhaps we should not need anything else to bring home to us the atrociousness of his death and the evil wrought by those responsible for it. But all down through the centuries the Church has discovered that images and figures can indeed help. And the image of the lamb being led to his slaughter has a power of its own in helping us to appreciate what was perpetrated on Christ and what he took, willingly and whole-heartedly, on himself. Generations of Christians from the beginning have taken the crucifixion to their hearts. It has been an enduring source of understanding for them, an insistent appeal to repentance, a comfort in their own suffering, a compelling lesson in true love and a means by which they can enter at a personal level into that love and seek to respond to it. It would be impossible to exaggerate the effect of Christ's passion and death on the Church, and on the minds, hearts, lives and devotion of countless individual Christians through every generation. And not just as something we contemplate with sympathy from outside but as an event in which we ourselves, all of us, are complicit. We were not there on Calvary that afternoon but in the figure dying on the cross we see the effect of sin; and the reality of our own sin will not allow us to ignore our share of responsibility for what was done to Christ there. This is what sin does. Christians of every age, looking at the cross, have had to accept their own role in that terrible event, but they have learnt too that they are beneficiaries of it and have drawn immense comfort, help and sense of purpose from what it achieved for us.

Is that Christian consciousness still as strong among us today? The reality of sin is increasingly ignored or denied altogether and this has its influence even within the Church. Our faith has become weaker and more reductive. We live in a culture of self-sufficiency, a culture that does not experience a need for faith or for forgiveness. Living in such a culture, Christians are inevitably influenced by it and share something of it, even unknowingly and unwittingly. We are children of our time.

Perhaps in the past in the Church of the West the emphasis on sin was too exclusive, overshadowing other aspects of our faith for many people. An increasing awareness of the overwhelming love of God for us has brought a new liberation and a new enrichment to the lives of many, as has the more recent growth in devotion to the divine mercy. These have helped us to take to heart the doctrine that our sins have already been overcome by Christ and indeed that they are already forgiven in him. But as is often the case in human affairs, in correcting one imbalance we are in danger of creating a new one. But our faith however is clear, and the cross, with its innocent figure dying in agony there, is an undeniable reality. If there is no sin, there is no place for a Saviour. Christ becomes just a man of good will and intent, who fell foul of the authorities and was put to death for it. An innocent man, perhaps, unjustly condemned and executed, but just one of many such in a world unable to find any meaning in innocent suffering; a world ultimately without hope.

This is not the Christ of Christian faith. St Paul speaks of some of his contemporaries as 'enemies of the cross of Christ' (Phil 3:18), and in that sense there are many of them today. But for one who contemplates the crucifixion with an open and responsive spirit, seeking to penetrate its meaning, seeking to find the truth that it reveals, seeking to understand the person of Christ and why he died in such an atrocious way, the cross with the figure nailed to it can provide its own answer and can lead those who approach it with a sympathetic spirit into its own mystery. The Lamb of God, the Lamb that was slain, by the power of his innocent death can draw us into the reality of his new life. This has been the experience of the Church from the very beginning.

Obviously, these last pages have ranged well beyond the natural limits of the figure of an innocent lamb put to death. But this is legitimate. The purpose of the image is to bring us more deeply into the reality, and the reality here is the innocent person of Christ subjected to an appalling and shameful death on the cross in order to reconcile God and humanity by restoring peace between them, and, in doing so, bring the forgiveness of sins and the salvation of the human race. It is an event that goes far beyond our limited understanding, but images such as that of the Lamb can speak to us in a different way, and often a more powerful one, than the workings of the discursive mind.

The author of the Apocalypse must have found this to be so, since, as we have seen, he continues to speak of Christ, now triumphant and risen to new life as the Lamb, the Lamb once slain who lives forever. The Lamb is an active figure, a central one, in the vision of heaven that the Apocalypse presents. There he is seated with the Father in glory. There, with the Father, he receives the honour, the recognition, the praise of the great company of heaven, the worship that he has won for himself – and won for us too, in the sense that we, his followers on earth, are caught up into it.

Back to the question with which we began. Lamb of God: what is the relationship between the Lamb and God? From what we have been seeing, we must say that the Lamb has certainly come from God, given to us for our salvation. But we must say too that the Lamb has come from our side and has offered himself to God for us and in our name. From both points of view, the Lamb belongs to God primarily. And it is clear throughout the Apocalypse that the Lamb is now seated with the Father in glory, and there, together with the Father and on terms of equality with him, receives the worship and the acclamation of all creation. In other words, the Lamb is not just from God for us and with God: the Lamb is God.

If we are to respect the true nature of the Lamb of God, as he has revealed himself in what he has done, we must recognise that all three interpretations are true of him. While 'the Lamb of God' is such a familiar and simple phrase in its form, it embraces truth both divine and human of the greatest depth and importance: the mystery of God and the mystery of our salvation.

The Body of Christ.
Amen

Five simple words in English, just three in Latin, but these ancient words have many layers there, levels of meaning and reference and allusion, and a great wealth of theology, spirituality and morality.

This is the body of the incarnation: the utterly unexpected way that God chose to be closer to his people, to make himself known to them, to enter more deeply into their lives as a people and as individuals, to engage more fully with the world. Utterly unexpected, but what better way could God have chosen to do this?

How do we get to know another person? Not just by listening to them but by observing them and interacting with them over the whole range of life. This is why God chose the incarnation: his people could get to know him through the life of his incarnate Son in this very human way, which was for them the very best way.

But it was not just a matter of God's making himself known to them. In its sin the human race needed more. Although it might not have recognised it, it needed a model of how we should live as God's people and in God's world. And it needed still more; it needed a Saviour, one who could reconcile it to God and overcome its alienation from him, its sin; one who could restore that peace to each of us, divided as we are right down to the depths of ourselves and of our existence. The Son of God came to us in a human body to create that at-one-ment with God and among ourselves, that all of us together and each of us individually seek.

God, of course, could have done all of this by a single act of the divine will, a fresh start, as it were. But this would not have respected the great project that God had planned in creating the human race and the world; it would not have respected the value, the dignity, that by God's gift we have in ourselves. God's salvation of the human race was not to be a merely external act of God's power exercised on us from outside. No, God's salvation would work from within, from inside ourselves and inside the world, painstakingly undoing all the evil that human beings had caused in themselves and in their world, and working on them through the human reality that is ours and through the natural processes of the world. In this way God would create humanity anew, as it were, from inside; God would restore humanity to its pristine state. But he would go further: God would prepare for himself a new people and a new world for the new future that was the aim of his plan.

Thus, in and through Jesus, the incarnate Son of God, humanity would be saved by one who was human; the human race would be fully involved in its own salvation.

And so, the human body of Christ will become the instrument of our salvation. It is the body in and through which Jesus will live a fully human life, an exemplary life, but in doing so he will draw on himself resistance, rejection, hatred, torture and a bitter death. In God's wisdom and his love, there was no other way to reconcile us with himself, with one another, with ourselves. 'Body', as I have been using it up to this, is not to be understood in a narrow, exclusive sense. Christ's body is his full human reality; it is himself present among us in a fully human, embodied way.

And this is the body too in which Christ rose from the dead, the body now completely transformed and now living with the Father in heaven, the body in which he will return in glory at the end of time.

The Eucharistic Body of Christ

It is also the body in which Jesus will make of himself a sacrificial offering to the Father on Calvary. It is the body in which at the Last Supper he anticipates this in a unique, sacramental way and so perpetuates for all the generations yet to come the memory and the power of what he will do the next day.

It is the body in which he gave himself in the form of bread to be taken and eaten, another completely unexpected choice and one that we have seen at greater length earlier in chapter ten. St Augustine says of it that, while in ordinary life we assimilate to ourselves the bread we eat and transform into our own bodily substance, in the eucharist it is that bread that assimilates us to itself and transforms us into its substance.[14]

So, when the eucharistic minister says to us as we approach to receive communion: 'The body of Christ', so much of the mystery of Christ is there in those simple words, all that we have been considering up to this point. And when we say 'Amen', we are giving our assent of faith: yes, I believe this, yes, I believe that this is indeed Christ's true body, yes, it is in this belief that I come to receive the Lord. It is a simple profession of faith between minister and recipient, a declaration of conviction and affirmation. And, while it takes place between one minister and one recipient, it is not a merely individual act. It is the faith of the Church, the faith of all of us who individually receive communion, but who do so together, in the communion of the Church and in our communion with one another.

No one can have all of this in mind while the minister is speaking and we are responding. But it is important for us to have some sense of the depth of truth and life in the gift that Christ has made to us of his eucharistic body. And it is important for us too to have some understanding of what we should really mean when we say our 'Amen'.

We have become used to the formulary 'The body of Christ. Amen', but it is worth recalling at this point that this form of words was introduced or restored to the Roman Rite only at about the time the Second Vatican Council was beginning. Up to then, the priest had said in Latin to each communicant, or as he moved between them: 'may the body of our Lord Jesus Christ keep your soul unto eternal life,' to which there was no response. The change was a welcome one. The new formulary is in fact a very old one, one that links us to the widespread practice of the early Church and one that pays the tribute of imitation to a long tradition of the Eastern Church.

The Ecclesial Body of Christ

There is still another layer of meaning which we have not touched on yet. *We* are the body of Christ. This we are by our baptism and this status is confirmed in the eucharist. As this body of Christ we eat the eucharistic body of Christ in order to become all the more the body of Christ. This is not a fanciful play on words. It is a truth that Paul recognised already in his first letter to the Church in Corinth, written about twenty-five years after the Last Supper: 'Because the bread is one, we, though many, are one body because we all eat of the one bread' (1 Cor 10:17), and he went on to criticise severely the community in Corinth for their conduct when they came together for the Lord's Supper. It was a desecration, the sort of conduct that was utterly unworthy of the body of Christ that they were and of the body of Christ that they received. He went even so far as to say that it was not the Lord's Supper that they were eating (1 Cor 11:20).

In time, this intrinsic ecclesial dimension of the eucharist became obscured in the Church of the West, but the use of the new eucharistic prayers in recent decades has been helping to shed once again the bright light of Paul's understanding and that of the early Church – never lost in the East – on our eucharist. Thus, Eucharistic Prayers II–IV pray that in partaking of the one bread and the one chalice, Christ's body and blood, we may become one body, one spirit in Christ by the Holy Spirit. The emphasis on unity is very clear; the fruit of the eucharist is to be the unity of those who share in it, the unity of the Church, a unity brought about by the body and blood of Christ and the power of the Holy Spirit working in them and through them.

For the Western Church the introduction of these new eucharistic prayers has proved to be one of the most enriching changes of the years following the Second Vatican Council. Until then we had only the Roman Canon, and, for all its venerability and its qualities, it made no mention of the role of the Holy Spirit or of the unity to be brought about by our sharing in Christ's body and blood. As a result, these were not a significant part of our understanding or of our spirituality. But now we have been given the opportunity and the incentive to broaden both. We have been learning to recognise more fully the inherently ecclesial dimension of the eucharist and to open ourselves to its consequences for ourselves as a community and as individuals. We have been learning too to enhance our understanding and our spirituality by welcoming in mind and heart the powerful pneumatological element that these have tended to lack. But that is ongoing work.

All of this is a rediscovery that we owe to the Second Vatican Council and the renewal that followed it. Of course, before this there had been heavy emphasis on the need for great reverence and for signs of reverence for the Blessed Sacrament, emphasis on the power and the effect of Christ's coming to us in the eucharist, emphasis on the need to prepare ourselves for this and on our need for prolonged thanksgiving after communion. This was one of the strong points of the eucharistic devotion of the time, but it tended to be narrowly individualistic: Christ, my Lord and my God, comes *to me* in his body. Of course too, we were very aware of our obligations to one another, to Christ's great commandment of love, but it was not linked closely in an ecclesial way with our reception of the eucharist or with the role of the Spirit there. The ecclesial and the pneumatological are closely linked here in the eucharist but our concern at this point is more with the former. A personal reminiscence will illustrate the distance that we have come in the fifty or so years since Eucharistic Prayers II–IV were introduced.

The textbook that we used while I was studying the eucharist, about 1960, had a full treatment of the eucharist as sacrifice and of its relation to Christ's once-for-all sacrifice, and a full treatment too of the nature of Christ's presence in his body and blood, of transubstantiation, and so on. And at the end of its lengthy presentation of these topics it had a sort of appendix, with a very brief reference, a couple of paragraphs, to what it called the 'social' aspect of the eucharist. I recall being disappointed, even at the time, sensing that there must be a better word to be found and a lot more to be said than this. (In 1960 we had not yet introduced or retrieved the word 'ecclesial', but that would follow soon.)

To recall this now gives us a mark of the great change over the years since then and of the rich blessings that God has been giving us in and through it. What must be a matter of deep regret, however, is that, in welcoming or at least accepting the new, many people have discarded so much of what was valuable in the old. But there is the larger contemporary phenomenon here of widespread dilution, or even, loss of faith.

Amen

When the eucharistic minister says to us: 'The body of Christ', it is not just the body of Christ's incarnation or his eucharistic body that the words designate. It includes in some way too his ecclesial body, the body that we are. And when we say: 'Amen', we are professing our faith in that too.

But 'Amen' is more than just an expression of assent; there is an element of commitment there too. So, when we respond 'Amen', as well as affirming our faith, we are committing ourselves to it too: Yes, I believe this and I will live by it; yes, I believe that I am a member of Christ's body and I will live as such a member should.

As so often, St Augustine has the words to express it. 'You are the body of Christ,' he says to his congregation, 'it is your mystery that is laid on the altar. You hear the words "The body of Christ" and you respond "Amen".' 'Be a member of the body of Christ,' he goes on, 'so that your "Amen" may be sincere.'[15] To which we add only one word: 'Amen.'

REMEMBER AND GIVE THANKS

already – not yet

The Eucharist in the Communion of Saints

Every time we say the Apostles' Creed, we acknowledge in faith the communion of saints. Obviously, it is a doctrine and a term with a long history in the Church. What does it mean? There is an ambiguity in the Latin *communio sanctorum*. It can mean what we usually take it to mean: the communion of God's people, *sancti* being understood here in the sense in which St Paul often uses it: those who have been called and sanctified by God in baptism and who live in accordance with their divine calling (for example, Rm 1:7; I Cor 1:2). But it can also mean, and this may well be the original sense it had, the communion of all who share in the holy things, that is, the eucharist in itself and as the culmination of the process of Christian initiation. This is illustrated in the Byzantine Divine Liturgy, where the priest, just before communion, proclaims: 'The holy things for the holy ones.' There is no opposition, no tension even, between these two possible interpretations: they complement each other. Over the centuries there has been a rich development, especially in the case of the first.

It is a communion created and sustained by God through baptism and the eucharist. And, as has been emphasised for a long time now, it is not confined to the Church in this world but extends to the Church in glory and to the Church saved but not yet in possession of the full life of that glory with God in heaven. This is a very real communion. We are united not just by thought or desire but in a much more objective way, and the heart of this is the person of Christ. We are united to him, he unites us to himself, in such a way that our union with him is an enduring reality within us; it is part of what we are.

St Paul has a very strong sense of this. From the beginning, he says, we have been chosen in Christ (Eph 1:4; 2 Th 2:13). It is a choice declared and achieved and made personal for each of us in baptism. Our life as Christians, as Paul keeps insisting, is a life in Christ. For Paul this is no vague or weak statement, no merely pious sentiment or aspiration. To say that we are in Christ is to state the truest and deepest thing about us; it is our real identity. We may understand it only very imperfectly, we may not feel it, but it is the hard reality of who we are in the depth of our being.

And because Christ has united us with himself in this way, by this fact he has united us in himself with one another. Again, there are many fellow Christians with whom we may feel no bond; with some, our relationship may be one of antipathy; some we may avoid or despise or even hate. But this does not alter what we all are before Christ. The Lord is not ignorant or dismissive of the shortcomings and faults and sins of each of us and of all of us. But what he sees when he looks at us is his great family of beloved sisters and brothers, a quarrelsome family, often divided, but one that he acknowledges as his own, one that he never ceases to love and to seek to transform.

This is the reality of the communion of saints: perfected in heaven, in the last stage of preparation for that perfection in purgatory, still a work in progress on earth. While we make these distinctions, we must recognise that the communion of saints is a single reality. The blessed in heaven are joined most intimately with us on earth, and we with them; those in purgatory too are united most intimately with us, and we with them. Indeed, dare we say that, at the level at which we are speaking, we are united with them even more intimately, now that they are dead, than we were when they were still with us here in this life? It must be so, since they are closer to Christ now than they were before, and, if they are closer to Christ, then, by that fact, they are closer to us than heretofore and we to them. This, of course, is not a fact of our experience, but it seems to follow from what it means for us to say that we, all of us together and individually, exist by God's grace in Christ. We can be so familiar with St Paul's phrase 'in Christ', that we do not always try to plumb the depths of the divine mystery beneath and behind the words.

What we have been saying about the relationship between the blessed in heaven and us here on earth and about the relationship between those being purified in purgatory and ourselves still on our journey, must we not say too, *mutatis mutandis*, about the relationship between the faithful in heaven and the faithful in purgatory? We are speaking here of something of which we have no experience, but must we not still say that the faithful in both of these branches of the Church continue to be joined in Christ and at a level of intimacy to which we on earth have not yet been raised?

We have tended to imagine heaven, I think, as a place sufficient unto itself and at a great remove from us; just as we picture God as infinitely above us, distant from our world. Of course, we are dealing with a mystery far beyond our comprehension here. God indeed is infinitely beyond us. But in the scriptures God has also revealed himself as very near to us, present in our world, in its history, its processes, its day-to-day life. God interacts with our world in a hands-on way: God is continuously guiding the world towards the fulfilment that he has planned as the culmination of his great divine project. And, likewise, must we not say something the same of heaven? The world of heaven intersects our world and is all around us. The saints are concerned for us in an active and effective way far beyond our understanding or our experience.

Can we not say something similar too of purgatory? Those in that state of purification have not lost their relationship with us, their fellow brothers and sisters in Christ. Death cannot simply have severed all the former ties of friendship and affection. In the communion of saints we are still of one family with them in Christ, and they with us. In the state in which they are, they will have a very different vision of things from what they once had or what we still do, a far deeper and truer appreciation of God and of ourselves, of what we are, together and individually, before him. And so, they must be more acutely aware than ever of our needs, and all the more eager to pray for us and to help in whatever way they can.

But we should remember too that, while from the beginning the Church has prayed frequently and consistently *for* the faithful departed, it has been reticent about praying *to* them. This is not to contradict what I have just been saying, but we are in the presence of a mystery that goes far beyond our comprehension and we must respect that as we search for a fuller understanding.

Offering the Eucharist in the Communion of Saints

What connections can we find between the communion of saints and the eucharist? We have seen earlier that the holy things of the eucharist, in themselves and as the sacramental climax of initiation, as its ongoing affirmation and renewal, are both the foundation and the living heart of the communion established among God's holy people who partake of them.

Who is it that celebrates the Mass? Ultimately, of course, it is Christ, but Christ makes his offering now through human agency. Since the Second Vatican Council we have been emphasising the celebrant assembly, people and priest gathered here and now, each carrying out their proper role, united in offering the eucharist to God. This was a truth that needed to be stressed in the situation of the time. Earlier, the emphasis had tended to be placed on the whole Church: it was the whole Church that made the offering through the action of Christ's ordained priest. At the time it was common for priests to celebrate the Mass with just the presence of a single altar server or even alone. Even in these circumstances he continued to say things like: 'The Lord be with you' (plural), and to respond: 'And with your spirit.' To whom was he speaking, and who was responding to him? The answer usually given was that he was addressing the whole Church and the whole Church was greeting him in reply. He was acting in communion with the Church universal and in its name.

Over recent decades we have retrieved the truth that the Church gathered here and now is celebrating this eucharist, this priest and this people united in fulfilling their respective roles. But this is not the whole truth, we must be careful that we do not now obscure the wider truth of the involvement of the whole Church in every eucharist.

All of this may sound merely formal and technical, little more than playing with words, but go behind the words to the truth they proclaim. Every eucharist is the doctrine of the communion of saints in action; in every eucharist it is present and is being lived out. From being a doctrine to be believed, it becomes a mystery that catches us up into its reality.

The Roman Canon (Eucharistic Prayer I), with its venerable history and its place at the heart of the Mass, recognises this: 'In communion with those whose memory we venerate, especially the glorious ever-Virgin Mary ... and blessed Joseph ... your blessed Apostles and Martyrs ... and all your saints.' It displays the understanding that, in making the offering, we are not just united with the Church on earth; we do so in communion with the saints in heaven, relying on their presence to us and their support as intercessors joined with us in our approach to God. Recall too the words of Eucharistic Prayer III, when it speaks of the saints, 'on whose constant intercession in your presence we rely for unfailing help'.

Others of our prayers express more freely and explicitly our request to God for the support of their intercession. To take a very clear example from the Liturgy of the Hours: in the memorial of the Blessed Virgin Mary on Saturday, as a response to the intercessions at Morning and Evening Prayer, we say: 'Lord, may your mother pray for us.' What can this mean? We seem to be asking the Lord Jesus, our one and great mediator, to prevail upon Mary to intercede with God for us. This cannot be so. But the prayer is there, along with a number of collects on the feasts of saints that seem to make a similar plea, even if not expressed so pointedly.

It may help to consider the question in the explicit context of the communion of saints. As we have seen earlier, the support of their intercession on our behalf is not something that we must wrest with difficulty from the saints, something conceded by them with a degree of reluctance, as if, to put it crudely, they felt it necessary to play hard to get. No, in the communion of saints their intercession is a given, offered to us and active in us before ever we ask for it. But, in God's plan, it is given as a gift to us by God, a gift on which we have absolutely no claim. Since we have no right of our own to it, we must never take it just for granted. The expression of this on our side is simple, humble petition, an open acknowledgment in appeal before God, made with thankful hearts. But it is a petition that we make with the fullest confidence; God has heard it and has granted it even before we present it. Indeed God granted it in advance in the very existence of the communion of saints. The close ties between the Church in heaven and ourselves in the communion of saints are a free gift of God's grace to us. This is an integral part of the outworking of the divine plan, an integral part of the way in which God carries his project forward towards its fulfilment.

We offer the eucharist then not as an isolated people or as a gathering of individual Christians; we offer it within the living, vibrant, engaged, active communion of saints and with all the support this gives us.

Prayer for the Church and the World
It is equally within the communion of saints that we pray in every eucharist for the great needs of the Church and that we pray for the world.

Frequently we are asked to pray for someone whom we do not know and with whom we have no personal connection. We do as we are asked, but our prayer may tend to be as for a stranger. The fact that we pray for Church and world in the eucharist can bring home to us that this prayer is not something extraneous to the eucharist; those we pray for are not somehow outside the eucharist, and what we seek for them is not something outside the eucharist or beyond its powers. Because of our relationship to them we owe it to the Church, we owe it to the world, to assist them with prayer. In the case of the Church, it is within the family of faith; in the case of the world, it is within the wider family of humanity. The Church, and we as part of it, are the universal sacrament of the salvation of the world, as the Second Vatican Council puts it. And what we ask God to grant them is a blessing within the scope of the eucharist, an effect of the mystery at its core. Those we pray for are not strangers, outsiders, but are, in God's eyes, in some relationship with the Church, and so with us, even if we may not be able to express this more precisely. We cannot understand fully God's great plan for Church and world, or its working out, or our contribution to its working out. We go by faith and with trust in God.

So, the communion of saints is actively and intimately involved in our celebration of the eucharist, involved with us in our making of the offering to God, involved in our offering of our petitions, and involved too in differing ways as beneficiaries of the offering and of the petitions we make in our communion with one another.

To pray for justice and peace in the world, to pray for unity among Christians, to pray for an end to violence and abuse in our society, may seem formal and abstract, a duty to be performed. But God sees all the peoples and communities and families and individuals who stand behind these generic words; people not distant from us, as we might imagine it, but people who are very close to us, even if we are not aware of it or of them. What we see as the great needs of Church and world can be very personal for all those who experience them, and our prayer, even if abstract in expression, in God's intent can be very concrete in its application. Such prayer is not optional for us; our brothers and sisters in Christ, the wider network of our sisters and brothers in our one world have a claim on us.

So too our prayer for the faithful departed. This is not just a category of humanity. These are people, many of whom we once knew and loved, and who remain very close to us in Christ, even closer perhaps than they were when they lived among us.

Broadening the Scope of Vision and Prayer

One of our most persistent temptations is to narrow our focus excessively on ourselves as individuals, on those closest to us, on our feelings, our standing before God, our sins, even our joy in the Lord. We must be concerned with all of these, of course, but not in any exclusive way, and here the breadth of the eucharist celebrated in the communion of saints has a great deal to teach us: if we are receptive, it opens our minds, our prayers, our lives to the great divine project, of which we are all part; it opens us to the fullness of the mystery that catches us up into that fullness as we celebrate the eucharist. We need to have brought home to us the hidden depths of our inmost being and the true dimensions of our existence in the world and of our life there. We are much more fully engaged with the world, its people, its needs than we imagine. In a culture of narrow and reductive individualism, the doctrine of the communion of saints together with the celebration of the eucharist has a lot to teach us and a lot to do for us.

In one of his works, Thomas Merton recounts an experience that he had at a busy intersection in an American city.[16] As he looked at the multitude of individuals who were moving there, intent on their business and largely oblivious of one another, he saw the bonds that connected them and somehow made a single people of them. But they passed one another and passed on their way, unaware of the unbreakable tie that bound them together and of the unity it created between and among them. The doctrine of the communion of saints, taken to heart and made our own, could create for us a similar insight of faith.

Living the Future
in the Present

You decide to go on a long journey. You know how far away your destination is and when you want to arrive there; you know how long you will stay. So you begin to make your preparations. The journey is still some days off, but already it is influencing what you are thinking and what you are doing here and now. It will determine at what time you must leave and what road you must take and what you need to bring with you. Your arrival at your destination is still in the future but already you are having to anticipate it in a variety of ways. The future is already determining the present for you and is already exercising its pull. Our life is full of many similar instances of the influence of the not-yet-existing future on the present.

It has been said of the liturgy that it is the future celebrated or realised in the present on the foundation of the past. And if it is true of liturgy in general, it is true of the eucharist in particular. All of life, the Christian must say, is lived in the tension of 'already' and 'not yet': what by God's grace we are even now in the present and what still awaits us in the future but is not yet ours; it is the future already with us and in us and the present not yet in our full possession of it. If we call it a 'tension' between them, it is a happy and challenging and fruitful tension.

For many Christians in the past, the promise of a life of peace and happiness with God in the world to come was a very real and powerful influence on them and on their lives. It was a promise that sustained them in hard times in all their suffering and gave them hope in an otherwise hopeless situation. And the same is true in the present for many whose life is a heavy burden. But that is not the way that a lot of people see it and experience it at present. They are more concerned with the here and now than with the future. It is interesting to note that, in a number of surveys of religious belief and practice over several years now, a surprisingly high proportion of those who call themselves Christian say that they do not believe at all in an afterlife. And among those who do profess such a belief, it has not the same place in their understanding or in their *modus vivendi* here and now. Some of them will say that they live as best they can in this world in the present: it is where we are and where we must live now, in the only time and in the only place available to us; the future, they feel, they can safely entrust to God.

As we saw earlier in chapters two and seven, when we Christians speak of the future as already at work in the present, we are not speaking of something completely beyond our experience, otherwise unknown to us, but for us as people of faith, the future is something a lot more real than that and it has indeed begun in us already.

The great project on which God is at work has a fulfilment in the future which God intends to accomplish and which God is preparing all through time. At the very heart of it is Christ, and through his life, death and resurrection Christ has already achieved that fulfilment in himself. He is now with God in glory, his humanity utterly transformed. But in God's design Christ was not just a single human being. Everything was created through him and for him, St Paul says (Rm 11:36; Col 1:16); all humanity is somehow joined to him and summed up in him by his incarnation and his paschal mystery. When he died, Paul says, we died with him and in him. When he rose from the dead and ascended into heaven, he raised us up with him and brought us with him to make us sit with him in glory; our life is hidden with him in God (Rm 6:1-11; Col 3:3). This, of course, is not a matter of experience for us but a reality of faith. If we are at some level even now with Christ in glory, then the future is not merely an expectation for us, however strong and heartfelt – it has begun, it is already present to us and at work in us in a real if inchoate way.

Christ is already the fulfilment in himself of our future; he has given us a pledge of this, but no ordinary pledge. Our pledge is the Holy Spirit, given to us as God's gift. Paul likens the Spirit to a sort of down payment, given us by God, an earnest of the payment in full that awaits us at the end, a guarantee of the fullness to be ours when we acquire possession of it (Eph 1:3-14).

For us in the present, this is a matter of hope, but Christian hope is a lot more than hope as we use the word in ordinary life; a lot more than mere optimism or desire or expectation. Our hope is rooted in Christ and the Holy Spirit and therefore it has in itself, in the present, the beginnings of its fulfilment in the future.

The Eucharist, the Future in the Present

To start where the eucharist started, at the Last Supper. This was more than a farewell meal of Jesus and his apostles, because, in his little ritual of bread and wine and the words he used that evening, Jesus anticipated the death that he would suffer on the following afternoon. What did his little ritual mean? Was he simply explaining to his apostles in a sort of prophetic gesture, a sort of catechetical lesson acted out in a ritual way, what was to take place the next day and what it would mean? There is surely more to it than that. He did not say: 'This will be my body ... my blood' but spoke in the present. In some way beyond our comprehension, he was already anticipating the reality of his death, already anticipating the great offering of himself to the Father that his death would consummate and seal, committing himself to it in advance, and giving his companions at table with him some participation in it already beforehand.

What he was doing that evening, with his chosen ones, they were to continue to do after him: 'Do this in memory of me,' he said (Lk 22:19; 1 Cor 11:24-25), do this as my memorial – not just an action by which he would be brought to mind in times to come but a memorial which would continue to make him and his sacrificial offering present through the centuries, so that his disciples of the future could participate in it, as the apostles were doing in anticipation on that first evening.

The circumstances of the Last Supper were unique, but the eucharist has continued ever since to be concerned not merely with the past but with its power here and now in the present, and with what it means for us and what it achieves and will achieve for us for the future and in the future.

In the eucharist it is the body in which Jesus lived his life and died and rose again that is present, offered to us now in all the glory of its transformed state, the body in which the future has been achieved and is fully present. This, of course, is a statement of faith and not of experience on our part. What it means is that, while the eucharist joins us to Christ's once-for-all sacrifice on Calvary from the past and while it brings us a living encounter with our great Saviour in the present, it does more: it makes the life of that future, now reached by Christ and fulfilled in him, present to us; it means that in receiving Christ's body and blood now we share already in that fullness, an anticipation for us and a foretaste of our own future.

But we have an infinitely better source of knowledge, true knowledge, than our human theologising – we have in the gospel of St John, as the words of the Lord himself, the simplest of words yet the most profound, in his discourse on the bread of life. One sentence in particular presents with great clarity the point I have been labouring over for several pages: 'Whoever eats my flesh and drinks my blood has eternal life and I shall raise him up on the last day' (Jn 6:54), present and future set neatly side by side. We are familiar with these words and, as Christians, we can accept very easily the promise for the future; it is the first part, so often in seeming contradiction of our experience of our life and of ourselves, that should take our breath away. Even now we have eternal life in and through the eucharist. If Christ had used the future tense here too, we would have had little difficulty in accepting what he said. But he put it in the present, and this poses a huge challenge to our understanding and to our full and unambiguous acceptance of its truth, because it is a truth too big for us.

What does the Lord mean by 'eternal life' here? He spells it out for us. Those who eat his flesh and drink his blood, he says, 'abide' or 'remain' in him, as he does in them. In receiving him we draw life from him, the life that he himself draws from the Father. The eucharist, then, gives us a true participation in the very life of God. What could heaven add to that, as far as eternal life is concerned? This is surely the very essence of the life of heaven, and it is ours now. It is eternal life, the eternal life that Jesus says we live by through his gift of his body and blood. And if we have eternal life even now, we surely have in that a promise of the same life in all its fullness and its splendour in the world to come. And Jesus says so explicitly: 'whoever eats this bread will live forever' (Jn 6:58), live forever in participation in God's own life.

Our concern here is with the life of the future, ours in the here and now and ceaselessly at work in us. We know that there may still be many years, with their good times and their bad, between us and that blessed fulfilment. But we know too, by faith, that we are called to live those years and all that they bring by the life of the Blessed Trinity within us. Through it all, that divine life will be working in us to make us ready for what God in the providence of his love has in store for us.

It is a great blessing to know from the Lord's teaching that we live by the life of the Blessed Trinity. But God, through Christ, is more generous still. It is to Christ that we owe this blessing and the fact that in him we live it, and Christ confirms this himself in our weekly or daily eucharist, where he comes to us in such a concrete, personal, intimate way and abides with us.

There are many challenging demands that all of this makes of us, but suffice it to pick out just a few here:

- A demand for thanksgiving, praise, blessing, glorification and worship of God. Eucharist means thanksgiving, thanksgiving in this more expansive, overflowing expression, and the Lord's gift to us of the eucharist is surely among his greatest and deserves a response from the very depths of a grateful heart.

- A demand that we move far beyond the lip service we often pay and grow in our eagerness to receive Christ's gift with ever-greater fruitfulness.

- A demand that we take Christ's words more deeply within us, so that they continue to nourish us with their life.

- A demand that we bring the truth of Christ's words and of his gift to bear on our daily lives, in order to bring richer meaning and purpose to those lives and to continue to transform them right up to the end.

Running through this is the need for desire on our part. We will not fulfil these demands by our own act of will or by our own power, but only with the help of God working with us. And these demands will take more from us than some vague wish or half-hearted desire. This is something we must *want*, really want.

This need for strong and determined desire from us is a common motif of St Augustine in his sermons. Such desire, for him, has the effect of expanding our capacity to receive. We desire something and by that fact we are making ourselves all the more eager and the more ready not just to receive but to appreciate and to welcome it. The stronger the desire on our part, the better we are prepared for what God wishes to give us.[17]

Underlying all of these is the demand for faith. It is faith that must be the foundation of all our eucharistic practice and reflection. At several points in his discourse on the bread of life, Jesus stresses the necessity of faith. And when many of his disciples rejected his words and left him, Jesus was prepared to let even those closest to him go too. It was Peter who rose to the occasion: 'Lord, to whom shall we go? You have the words of eternal life and we believe; we know that you are the Holy One of God' (Jn 6:68-69). It was a magnificent response, and we must hope that his words speak for us too.

Life, Death, Love

Christianity is a religion of paradox, indeed of contradiction, must we not say? The first will be the last and the last first. Whoever loses his life keeps it, whoever keeps his life loses it. The master will be the one who serves, the one who is prepared to go on his knees before his servants and wash their feet. And so on. Christ's words are full of such paradoxes, as is his own life, because he himself lived by the message he proclaimed. At his presentation in the temple on the fortieth day after his birth, Simeon spoke of him as 'a sign of contradiction' (Lk 2:34), and his later life confirmed this. He took the wisdom of human experience and reflection and stood it on its head.

If Christ is such, then such must be the Church of his disciples, and such must be its gospel, and such must be the lives of his individual followers.

There is a paradox of this kind at the heart of the eucharist, the greatest paradox of all. Eucharist, as we know, means thanksgiving, and that is how it presents itself there, a great act and prayer of thanksgiving to God for all that he is in himself and all that he has done for us. Eucharist here is to be taken in a broad and full sense. It is thanksgiving that overflows into blessing and praise of God, into confession of his name, into acknowledgment of all his gifts to us. The range of words used is extensive. The Mass then is an occasion of great joy and delight.

But here is the beginning of the paradox. At the heart of all that God has done for us we place the death of Christ, his Son – not any ordinary human death but one of great cruelty and suffering and humiliation and shame. And while we recognise this as something evil, perpetrated by the forces of evil among us in defiance of God, we see it also, and at a deeper level of truth, as God's will, accepted in obedience and faithfully carried through by Christ right to the bitter end.

We need to take in the full reality of this before moving on. How could the hideous scene of Calvary be a matter for thanksgiving, a matter for the joy that accompanies thanksgiving, even when viewed retrospectively and with a broader vision? How can we rejoice when what faces us is an act of such profound suffering and evil?

We express our thanksgiving and our joy at greater or lesser length in the words of the eucharistic prayer. But by Christ's gift we go beyond words. After the institution narrative and consecration of the Mass, the language of offering becomes more explicit and more pointed. We speak of offering to the Father the sacrificial oblation that Christ made of himself, and this not just as an event from the past but as a living reality made present to us every time we celebrate the eucharist in Christ's name. Thus, Eucharistic Prayer III says: 'We offer you in thanksgiving this holy and living sacrifice.' All our thanksgiving is first God's gift to us, as Common Preface IV reminds us, but this is true especially here in its very highest level and expression. Our thanksgiving takes the form of offering, an offering given to us by God: the original sacrifice of Christ made present to us by God's act here and now in sacramental form in our celebration of each eucharist.

Thus there is at the core of the eucharist the paradox that the highest expression of our joy in our God – our delight in his love – is the figure of Christ, tortured, reviled, abandoned, dying in public ignominy on the hill of Calvary.

Are we giving thanks to God here for sin, for evil, as it manifested itself in so many ways in Christ's passion and death? We are certainly coming very close to it, but it cannot be for the sin simply in itself; it is for the love with which Christ engaged with it, the love with which he endured the force of its power – a diabolical power – and of its effects; endured them in himself, and, by enduring, overcame that power in its very source. In God's great design, this was the only way by which victory could be won. It is for all of this that the eucharist gives thanks to God. And, of course, we give thanks for the blessed outcome, in Christ in the first place, and in ourselves too with Christ and in him.

In the scene of Calvary we see the power and the effects of human sin, but what took place there that afternoon was not just a manifestation of human evil, however depraved. It was a manifestation of the power of diabolical evil, the still greater and more powerful evil that uses all the forms of human sin for its own nefarious purposes, in its hatred of God and its rebellion against him. Christ's struggle, as we see it in his passion, was with human sin in all its reality and with its all-pervasive effects, but at a still deeper level it was with the diabolical power that prompts and uses and works through that human sin. It should be no surprise to us that the human nature of Christ, faced with the decisive battle against such a power of evil, far surpassing the human, should have shrunk from it in fear and trembling, as Christ's did in the garden of Gethsemane. This should alert us rather to the nature of the struggle confronting him.

Jesus had a preliminary encounter with this evil in his temptations at the beginning of his public ministry. On that occasion, as St Luke tells us (Lk 4:13), Satan left him to return at the appointed time, a time that surely came now in his agony in the garden and throughout his passion, as it unfolded.

It will take a force of the greatest power to transform the horror of the scene at Calvary and what led to it. But there was such a power, an utterly unexpected power, and it was of an altogether different kind from the weapons of human ingenuity or the more subtle weapons of Satan. It was love, Christ's love, God's love.

When we look at Christ's cross with the eyes of faith, we must learn to see there a great act of divine love: the love of the Father in willing it, the love of the Son in his submission to it – not a forced or reluctant acquiescence on his part but an eager and whole-hearted act undertaken and persevered in out of love. Jesus handed himself over to death, as the scriptures make clear, but we must say too that at the deepest level of the mystery of the cross it was in order to fulfil the Father's will. 'God so loved the world that he gave his only Son, so that all who believe in him may not perish but may have eternal life' (Jn 3:16). The Father, who gave his Son to the world in his incarnation, continued to give his Son all through his life, and thereby handed him over to the consequences of his perfect obedience to the Father, even his passion and death, whatever the circumstances in which these might take place. In the Letter to the Philippians, we read, he 'was humbler yet, even to accepting death, death on a cross' (Phil 2:8). And in his passion Jesus accepted this, as he accepted his Father's will in everything. He aligned his will with the Father's and in obedient love lived it through to the end.

This is how we continue to understand Christ's cross, as an act of extreme barbarity on the part of those responsible for it, but, deeper than that and beyond it, as a supreme act of divine love, carried through with matching love by Christ, God's Son. And we acknowledge too that we are not casual or innocent observers at Calvary, looking on with distaste or in horror at what is being done before our eyes. Somehow, we too are complicit in it all and we cannot wash our hands of it. Christ in his death in agony on the cross is the last word of human sin; he is the proof of the reality and the power of evil. However, there is a word of far greater power at work there too; a word that changes the scene of Calvary and transposes it to an altogether different level. Because Christ in agony is also the word spoken by God, God's final word, a word of life, a word of compassion and mercy and forgiveness and love.

But we have to face in all seriousness the fact that ultimately God allowed his beloved Son to be handed over to death on our behalf, allowed him to be subjected to the power of his unjust judges and his torturers and executioners. And we believe that God did this solely out of love for us, his wayward family. This is a truth that goes far beyond the limits of our understanding, and we recognise this when we are confronted by it. How can the Father, any father, do such a thing to his Son? How can such an act on a father's part be an act of love? How can it be equally an act of love on the Son's part in his accepting it? At a time when we set such store by personal freedom, it seems grossly offensive even to suggest it. But the testimony of scripture is clear: this is what the Father did, and it was an act of love, the supreme and all-surpassing love of God. It shows the value that God places on his world of creation, on the human race as a whole, and on each of us, its individual members. In God's great design, we in all our weakness, our ugliness and our repeated sin are worth the death of his own Son. It is a truth that our human reasoning and our theological reflection can help us to recognise and accept only at quite a superficial level. It will take God's special grace and gift, working through contemplation, to carry us into the true, life-giving riches of the mystery.

There is one effect, an essential one, which we have not mentioned yet. Christ's life did not end with his redemptive death. We believe that he rose from the dead, raised up by the Father through the power of the Holy Spirit. And we believe, as a consequence, that in some sense we too rose with him, in the same act and by the same power of our God. Our Christian faith will never allow us to break the bond between Christ's death and his resurrection and we must give due attention to each. On the one hand, we must accept that the Christ who died on the cross passed through his bitter death to the glory of his resurrection. We cannot allow our vision or our understanding or our reflection to stop at his death on Calvary. But we must also accept, on the other hand, that if Christ is now seated with the Father in glory, utterly transformed, this is only because he first had to die his painful and ignominious death in order to pass through to the triumph of his resurrection. There was no other way. His passion and death with all their intense suffering bring him to his new life of glory; and this new life of glory is attained by him only through that intense suffering. This is the full reality of the paschal mystery.

However modest the setting in which it may be celebrated and however simple the ritual, it is this mystery in all its riches that is the core of our eucharist. The dynamic of the celebration carries us beyond our words of thanksgiving into real participation in and engagement with Christ in the unfolding of his sacrifice, and through him with the Father and the Holy Spirit: in other words, participation in and engagement with life and death and with the love at work in them. Life, death, love – that is the mystery that is the core of the eucharist and, more broadly, the core of our Christian faith and our Christian existence.

Our temptation is to allow our familiarity with the eucharist and its very ordinariness, so to speak, to dull our vision and to impede the effort of faith that its true celebration demands of us. And so, we close ourselves to its deeper levels and to the surpassing wealth that it offers us for our understanding and for the apparent ordinariness of our day-to-day living, our daily round. But there is nothing ordinary about a life which must end in either eternal blessedness or personal disaster, and that is every human life. There is nothing ordinary about a life in which the love of God is present, a life inspired by Christ and rooted in him. This is the life that, while it will bring many small deaths, is already in us, by God's grace, the beginning of our life with Christ in the glory of the world to come.

The Reserved Sacrament

It has been said of the Blessed Sacrament that it is 'the Mass held in meditation', a prolongation, as it were, of the time between the institution narrative and consecration and communion, and it is easy to see why. The Sacrament comes to us from within the Mass and is reserved in order to extend the grace of the Mass beyond the time and place of its celebration. The original reason for what we now call reservation seems to have been so that the dying could be provided for in their special need. And in the early centuries too we hear of people in some places taking the Sacrament home with them. Later, there will be stories of some missionaries and pilgrims bringing the Blessed Sacrament with them on their journey.

Veneration and reservation of the Blessed Sacrament did not begin in the Middle Ages. In the early Church there is evidence for prayer addressed to Christ in the time between the institution narrative and consecration and the communion. (St Augustine, for example, insists that Christ's flesh be adored before it is eaten[18] and in the seventh century the *Lamb of God* was introduced to accompany the breaking of the bread.) We should note that such forms of devotion emerge first from within the liturgy itself. There is striking evidence likewise for the recognition that Christ remains present in the Sacrament even after Mass is ended and so is to be venerated there. Any disrespect towards the Sacrament is severely condemned. Practices such as these are in place long before the development of extra-liturgical forms in the Middle Ages. There is no need to multiply examples. These practices and others like them arise out of and bear witness to the belief, already firmly established in the Church from the earliest centuries, that Christ is present in his eucharistic body and remains present even after the eucharist has been celebrated.

From early in the ninth century, new and sharp questions began to be asked in the Church of the West about the precise nature of Christ's presence in the eucharist. Christ is indeed present, but what we see before our eyes and taste and feel is bread. How are these to be reconciled? There were those who, in insisting on the reality of that presence, used a language of great realism, thus exposing themselves to the charge that what they were arguing for was a grossly material understanding of that presence – a capharnaitic sense, after the reaction of many of Christ's disciples when they rejected the conclusion of his discourse on the bread of life at Capernaum. But their opponents in their turn were accused of denying the full reality of Christ's presence in the eucharist.

It took a couple of centuries of rather scrappy debate for a language to emerge that would profess the full reality of Christ's presence, while at the same time preserving it from the dangers of an extreme and gross realism. It was in this context that the use of the word 'substance' began to spread, and this then led on to 'transubstantiation', which made its appearance in the twelfth century and established itself very firmly in the centuries that followed.

One of the major effects of this was to focus attention even more sharply on the person of Christ truly, really and substantially present in all the fullness of the mystery of his being.

All of this led to a rapidly increasing emphasis on the Sacrament reserved, on the receptacle that contained it and on its place in the church, on the worthiness of both for so great a sacrament. This was accompanied by a corresponding increase in the signs of respect and of veneration paid to the Lord present there. From early in the thirteenth century a practice of elevating the host at the institution narrative and consecration of the Mass spread very quickly, followed a century later by the elevation of the chalice. There developed a great desire among congregations generally to see the host ('the gaze that saves'). Later in the same century the feast of Corpus Christi was introduced and was very widely celebrated in the Western Church.

All of this gives us the context from which enhanced veneration of the Blessed Sacrament began to emerge, giving rise to special worship and to the extended practice of prayer before it. The awareness of Christ's presence in the eucharist was greatly strengthened and this presence there became over time the focus of different forms of devotion, such as exposition, blessing with the Sacrament and processions.

It should be remembered that all this time what we came to call 'Holy Communion' was very infrequent at Mass. We may ask the question, even if we cannot answer it satisfactorily: how much of what we have been describing was a way of filling up what was lacking in people's experience of the Mass? People were no longer participating in the ways that they once did, and by now this practice of infrequent communion was very widespread and had been long established. Such were the prevailing conditions in which a variety of forms of public veneration of the reserved Sacrament developed, and, following closely on this, a deep, warm, personal devotion to the person of Christ present there.

These practices and this devotion were given fresh vitality through the eucharistic controversies of the Reformation period and of the following centuries. The Catholic Church vigorously defended its belief in what it came to know as the 'Real Presence', and this in turn led to a further strengthening of eucharistic devotion, to the emergence of new forms and the development and expansion of existing ones (Forty Hours, prolonged exposition, personal visits to the Blessed Sacrament, for example). Religious congregations were founded that had eucharistic devotion as their inspiration and the core of their lives.

This devotion, at the centre of the Church's life over such a long time, has brought great benefit to the Church and blessings beyond counting into the lives of so many of its people.

Now we are in a time of widespread, rapid and profound change once again, changes that affect eucharistic devotion and its many expressions in a critical way. From early in the twentieth century until after the Second Vatican Council, one of the great pastoral efforts was to restore frequent and even daily communion. The changes introduced by the Council aimed to bring about greater active participation, both outward and interior, in the celebration of the eucharist. Just as there may have been some element of compensation for the absence of these in the emergence and the long duration of such a vital devotion to the person of Christ present in the Blessed Sacrament, so we must expect changes in the new situation of today. Of course, other, broader factors – weakening of faith, decrease in prayer, competition from secular attractions – are at work here. We are losing a great deal that was good in the situation we inherited.

It seems clear that our traditional eucharistic devotion will no longer have the vital, central role that it had for so long in the Church. Much of it will change, must change, but we cannot acquiesce passively in its continuing decline towards virtual disappearance. We must work on our understanding of Christ's presence there and how we preach, teach and present it. We must remember that reservation of the Blessed Sacrament arises from the celebration of the Mass and aims to extend the grace and blessings of the Mass beyond the time and the place of the celebration. Attention to this fact can help to inform and to revitalise our eucharistic devotion and its forms; it can allow the great themes of the Mass, firmly centred on Christ in the sacrifice of his death, to bring fresh life to our veneration of the Blessed Sacrament and at the same time can allow the warm and personal quality of our veneration to feed back into the faith and the devotion that we bring to the Mass.

Communion is not just a part of the Mass. It draws us in its own unique way into the totality of what the Mass celebrates: Christ's death, which issued in his resurrection, as the sacrifice of our redemption, the wider divine plan of salvation, the Lord's enduring presence, the gift of the Spirit, forgiveness and new life, the mystery of the Church, thanksgiving and praise, etc. We cannot make all of this our own in the short time that the Mass takes and the even shorter time after communion. We need to discern too what effect our weekly or daily eucharist should be having on our lives when we leave the church.

We go together as Christ's body to receive from the Lord by the hand of his minister the bread from which the Church draws its life. It is a communal act, but Christ comes to us individually there; he comes to each of us in a most personal way. Again, in the time available to us there is not the opportunity to prolong these few minutes of concentrated attention to Christ, of faith-filled and warm devotion.

We must identify which forms of this devotion can survive in a healthy way into the future and how these can be renewed or transformed to restore their vitality. And we must strive to find new forms that will bring us closer to the person of Christ living among us in the Sacrament.

We may hope and pray that the Lord among us will bring new out of the old, but, as always, we must keep giving him something on which to work. We cannot afford to lose such a source of blessing, so much that was good, in what has been passed on to us. We cannot allow our eucharistic faith to be diluted or otherwise weakened. Now is a time when we are being urged insistently and repeatedly by Church leaders to place the living Christ at the heart of our Church life, of its preaching and of our own individual lives. There is too much at stake here for indifference or lack of effort.

Through Christ our Lord. Amen

'Through Christ our Lord': Is there a phrase more familiar to us than this in all our liturgy? Is there a phrase that goes more quickly and more deeply to the heart of the liturgy? And yet, its very familiarity has brought one great drawback: we do not really hear it anymore, we do not listen to what it is saying, we do not allow it to bring us into the riches or the power of the truth that it expresses.

When the priest comes to the words 'Through our Lord Jesus Christ' in the collect of the Mass, we know that the prayer is ending. This is our formulary of conclusion, the Church's way of bringing it to an end, and we switch off. So, the congregation prepares to be seated, the reader begins to come forward, and the priest relaxes his concentration – he knows this part of the prayer by heart.

All of this is a great pity because we are missing what may well be the most important part of the prayer, at least in that it is these words that make explicit the very foundation of this prayer, as of all our prayer. These words invoke before the Father the mediatory role of Christ. This it is that sustains our prayer and gives it its true value and power.

Behind the words 'through Christ our Lord' there stands the doctrine that Christ is our mediator. St Paul gives this doctrine its classic expression: 'There is one God; and there is one mediator between God and humankind, Christ Jesus, himself human' (1 Tm 2:5). In the incarnation the Son of God became man. And so, in him divinity and humanity are brought together in a unique way in one person. Jesus can truly represent God to us and us to God. In his humanity he can bring God to us, and in that human life and human death we can see and we can encounter God in a fully human way. In the divine plan, it is in and through Christ in his humanity that God comes to us, and in and through him that we are given access to God.

That humanity of Christ has now been glorified and is seated with God in majesty, and in that humanity Christ continues to represent us to God and to intercede for us. Christ understands through and through from his own experience what it means to be human, because he himself has lived our life and died our death, and out of that experience he can intercede for us with deeply personal understanding and sympathy.

Closely allied to this, another expression of it is the doctrine of the priesthood of Christ, so extensively and so skilfully presented in the Letter to the Hebrews. By God's appointment, Christ in his humanity is a priest, our unique priest. He was a priest all through his life on earth and in that time he learned what it is to be human, learned to sympathise with us in our weakness because he himself shared in that weakness. 'He was tempted in every way that we are, though without sin' (Heb 4:15), the author says, like us then in all things but sin. It brought him to his experience of death, and his great priestly act was his offering of himself to the Father in death.

This was not the end of his work as a priest because his humanity is now in glory with the Father forever, and there he continues his intercession on our behalf and will go on doing so: 'ever living to intercede for us' (Heb 7:25). In God's design, it is not an outsider, an angel, say, whom we have to represent us; it is one of our own, one who knows us from the inside, one who has been through it all himself. To believe this must be a source of great comfort, encouragement and confidence for us in our own experience and in the sharp awareness of our need.

Our prayer then is made through this living Christ; it is caught up into the powerful intercession of our priest in heaven and is presented before the Father as his prayer, made on our behalf.

If we leave our consideration of Christ's mediatory role at that, we are neglecting one important dimension of it. When we think of Christ as Mediator, we think of the part he plays in presenting our intercession to the Father.

But do we not say in every Mass: 'always and everywhere to give you thanks ... through Christ our Lord' or similar words? Prayer is not limited to petition, and the prayer of the blessed in heaven is very largely an expression of thanksgiving, praise, worship, adoration, blessing and acknowledgment of our all-holy God. We have striking instances of this in the Apocalypse, in the songs placed on the lips of the blessed, as these are used on many occasions in the Evening Prayer of the Liturgy of the Hours (Apoc 4:11, 5:9, 10, 12, 11:17-18, 12:10-12, 15:3-4, 19:1-2, 5-7). During his time on earth, Christ offered such prayer to his Father out of the fullness of his heart and his experience, and he unites his Church with himself in pouring it out ever since before the Father. He catches us and our prayer up into his own great heavenly canticle of thanksgiving and praise, and thereby gives it a value and a dignity that it could never have of itself.

All of that is summed up in the simple words 'Through Christ our Lord', whether it is the prayer of the Church or the prayer of the individual Christian. There is another aspect that we should not overlook. The words are not saying merely that it is through Christ that we are making our prayer. Are they not saying too that it is our hope and our confident expectation that God will hear them and that we shall have our answer, because of the power of Christ's intercession?

And then there is the 'Amen', a throwaway word much of the time, we may fear, another victim of familiarity. But it is a word of great depth and density, a word of great strength. It is a word that Jesus himself used frequently when he wished to give emphasis to what he was saying.

As a response from the congregation to the prayer that has preceded it, it means: Yes, this is indeed our prayer and we are making it our own; what the words ask for, we ask for; and we too join in seeking the intercession of Christ as we offer the prayer.

I have said elsewhere, in chapter 14, that there is an element of commitment in our 'Amen', as if to say: we will accept the blessings God gives in answer and we will respond to them and use them well.

Of course, we cannot have all of this in mind while the prayer is being spoken and we are responding. But it can be part of the understanding and of the conviction that we bring to the eucharist. It can be part of the general awareness of faith that informs our Christian life and animates our prayer.

A final point on this matter: There should never be anything to suggest that Christ's role is understood in a rather mechanical, detached way. Nor is he to be seen as a sort of higher grade heavenly postman, who gathers the letters given to him and delivers them safely and unopened to the Father. No, Christ, our mediator, is personally and fully engaged in what he does. He makes our petitions his own and offers them as his own to the Father. In receiving our prayers Christ engages with us fully too, and that is why our prayer through Christ should have in it a silent prayer, a movement of the heart, to him. Prayer through Christ encourages and includes prayer to him.

The Intercession of Mary and the Saints

There is an ancillary matter, related to our main theme, which perhaps should be touched on here. At another place in these pages (chapter 15) I have written on the communion of saints. The Church has long had the conviction that the saints intercede for us and support our prayer to God. This conviction has remained strong all down through the centuries. And among the saints a special place has been recognised for the intercession of the Blessed Virgin Mary. In parallel with this, there has been the conviction all through that the entire Church on earth intercedes for its members and joins with them in supporting their prayers.

But if we have only one mediator, Christ, how is this wider intercessory role of the Church on earth and in heaven to be understood in relation to his? One point is very clear from the start: nothing that we say about the Church's intercession may interfere with or obtrude on the unique role of our one mediator, the man Christ Jesus, or on the perfect adequacy of what he does.

To acknowledge the intercessory role of the saints and of the Church and the special role of Mary implies no deficiency in Christ's work, as if to suggest that it required this supplementary assistance. If there is a role for other forms of intercession, as there is, this can only be in complete subordination to Christ's, and indeed be an aspect of his and a result of it.

This issue arises more sharply for us in the intercession of Mary and the title frequently given to her, especially in more recent times: Mediatrix of all graces. However this is to be understood, it cannot mean that Mary is somehow our co-mediator with Christ before the Father. If we are justified in calling her mediatrix, it is the effect of Christ's will and the fruit of his work. I labour this point because the accusation has often been made by some of our fellow Christians that in its devotion to Mary, or at least in some of its popular manifestations, and in the sort of language it uses of her, the Catholic Church denies or at any rate obscures the truth of Christ's unique and all-sufficient role.

There seem to be a few voices at present suggesting that access for us to Mary is through Joseph. It is as if we are dealing with a heavenly bureaucracy, in which every request has to be made through the proper channels and be passed up through the various levels until it reached the top. This, of course, is absurd. Christ is our unique mediator, and, while the intercessory roles of Mary and of the saints and of our fellow members of the Church on earth is very real, it is by Christ's will; the fruit, in some way, of Christ's unique role and an expression of it. We all pray for the Church and for the world and for one another, and in the prayers of Mary and of the saints we can recognise a special efficacy because of the special holiness of their lives; this is the result of Christ's own work in them and of the quality of their cooperation with it. But Mary and the saints and other holy people are standing at our side, one with us in making our prayers to Christ and through him to the Father. They are not, as it were, standing with Christ and at his side to receive our prayers. We can relate this to the communion of saints, which we have considered elsewhere. This is the communion of saints at work, so to speak, engaging and revealing in what it does the depths of what it is.

Nothing that I have been saying over the last page or so should be thought to imply that there is anything dubious about the Church's belief in the intercessory role of the saints, about the special place of Mary in it, or about the general practice that arises from it. It is a truth that has proved to be a great comfort to countless Christians down through the centuries, a truth that has brought them closer to the Lord Jesus, closer to God, a truth for us to rejoice in and to welcome into our life of faith.

We should not allow the intricacies and the arguments of the last few pages to obscure the true reality and the mystery of prayer in the Church. All of the aspects of this that we have been exploring should open our minds and our hearts to the riches of prayer in God's design and by his grace, and the riches that our own prayer, poor and feeble as we know it to be, can rely on and draw on and share in.

In prayer, we are never alone. But too often we do not appreciate this; our eyes can be closed to the blessings around us, to the height and depth and the breadth of the mystery of our Christian prayer and our Christian life.

But even there God is full of compassion for us in our weakness, as is Christ our mediator, and he can work within us in his own way, usually hidden from us, to bless us with all the abundance and the generosity that are his.

Afterword

Liam M. Tracey OSM

The reform and renewal of the celebration of the liturgy has been one of the most obvious and lasting consequences of the Second Vatican Council (1962–5). While this task has continued until the present day, and some would argue that it has only really begun with many stops and starts along the way, the antecedents of the work of the Council stretch back to the beginning of the twentieth century and even before.

The Modern Liturgical Movement is rightly regarded as one of the great contributory factors to the work of the Council and its desire to reform and renew the worship of the Church. With the address of the Benedictine monk, Lambert Beauduin to an assembly of young Catholic workers in Malines (Belgium) in 1909, and his call for active and conscious participation in the liturgy and a realisation that the liturgy and its celebration is the true piety of the Church, the movement was regarded as beginning its work. The book you have just read by Patrick McGoldrick is profoundly rooted in this movement and its impact on liturgical reform and renewal flowing from the Council. Key to this task has been the rediscovery of the history and theology of the liturgy in the lives of Christian communities past and present. The renewal of liturgy is not just an archaeological exercise as it has often been accused of being, but an ever-deeper immersion in the best of the Christian tradition. Part of coming to a knowledge of that tradition is an ever-greater appreciation of the role of the history and theology of the liturgy itself. One of the great blessings of the last century and more of the Modern Liturgical Movement and the movements in renewing our appreciation of Scripture and Early Christianity, is our growing knowledge of the development of the liturgy itself. Closely allied to the Modern Liturgical Movement has been the Ecumenical Movement. Indeed, Beauduin is a key figure in both these blessings of the last century.

As Christians met together in prayer and sought to fulfil the prayer of the Lord that they all be one, they grew in their knowledge of each other's traditions, especially that of their worship. Tradition comes to be seen as so much broader than just the expression of one particular Church. From the Churches of the Reform, Catholics gained a greater appreciation of the Word of God and its preaching. The importance of hymnody in the shaping of the Christian faith and the constant call not to break the links between discipleship, worship and care for the world in which we live and all its people are central to the Reformed tradition and a constant challenge to other communities. In coming to know the Churches of the East, many Western Christians met for the first time a very different way of worshipping. From the use of icons and a very different style of Church music to texts that brought worshippers back many centuries, Catholics especially were taken back to the first millennium and before. Many of their concerns in liturgy they found were not the preoccupations of these Churches and the liturgical theology of these Churches was profoundly linked to the way they worshipped. Some of these Churches reached back to the very earliest Christian communities and their Semitic origins. We learnt that there was more than one eucharistic prayer, that there were many prayers. Crucially the role of the Holy Spirit was central in eucharistic theology, and the emphasis on the words of institution was not to be found in these traditions. This knowledge is growing all the time, and as scholars publish their latest findings, and, some of what we thought we knew needs to be revised and reassessed. So it is with this volume. This afterword is designed to present some recent research on the origins, development and celebration of the eucharist, the central Christian act of thanksgiving and some suggestions for further reading.

The search for the origins of Christian worship was relatively late in studying the Jewish milieu out of which the Christian movement was born. Previous scholars believed that the earliest generations of Christians would have rejected or radically transformed the patterns of worship with which they were most familiar. What has become increasingly clear is that this is not an accurate view. It is now widely accepted that the roots of many Christian practices, including those of worship, are found in the Jewish origins of Christianity. However, it is not an easy task to decipher what may well be links between the two and what may be not. This is not just limited to the issue of the Jewish origins of the Christian movement it also affects how the relationship(s) between Christianity and Judaism is seen today, especially in the light of the Shoah, or the Holocaust. Nothing Christians do or say about Judaism should promote anti-Semitism.

This means there has to be an understanding that Christians and Jews read the scriptures in a different way. While Christians call the scriptures known by Jesus and his earliest followers the 'Old Testament', for many contemporary Jewish believers 'Old' is understood to refer to the past and therefore to be no longer useful or valid. As a Jewish rabbi once told me, 'For you it may be old, but for me it is always new.' Clearly, for Judaism there is no 'Old Testament'. Their scriptures are formally, 'the Law, the Prophets, and the Writings' (Torah, Nevi'im and Ketuvim) making up the term Tanakh, which is used as a label for these writings. The key for Christians of course is that they read the two testaments in the light of the life, ministry, death and resurrection of Jesus. This is clearly not the case for Judaism. Some Christians now call the first testament, 'Hebrew Scriptures' or 'Hebrew Bible'. This is to avoid the confessional term 'Old Testament'. What is important is that the Christian reading of the scripture must not promote or denigrate Judaism. Reading the scriptures purely in terms of promise and fulfilment can give the impression that Christianity, and more especially the Church, has totally replaced and taken the place of the people of Israel.

Much of what liturgical historians have written on these topics has been built on outdated Jewish liturgical scholarship that saw links where there were none, and used texts and practices from much later periods, reading them back into these formative centuries. Rarely did they think that these influences could be mutual, that Christian practice also influenced Jewish worship. It is only in the last thirty years that a more nuanced viewpoint has begun to emerge. Crucial to this understanding is how the relationship between Christianity and Judaism is conceived. We need to move beyond an approach of a Jewish parent and a Christian child image to seeing early Christianity and nascent Rabbinical Judaism as unruly siblings born from Second Temple Judaism. Important to note in this changing view of Christian and Jewish origins is that there is not one Judaism at this point, just as there is not one form of Christianity, there are many different groups and sects.

Like their Christian counterparts, Jewish liturgists now see Jewish liturgy as changing and developing to the new circumstances in which the Jewish people found themselves after the destruction of the Jerusalem Temple in 70 CE. This fundamental event profoundly shapes Jewish practice and prayer. It is in this period after the loss of the temple, that the structure of the synagogue and its liturgy takes shape. Different Jewish groups shape these structures and we are learning it was not just the Pharisees who are active in this task. While there may well have been gatherings in synagogues before 70 CE, they were more akin to Scripture study sessions than liturgy. These gatherings for study of the Law lasted many hours and varied from place to place. It has been noted that synagogues were much more akin to community centres than places of worship at this point. It is only later that prayer texts, orders of service, festivals and the place of worship itself are fixed as the role of the rabbi as a community leader and a figure of authority becomes more defined. Flexibility gives way to uniformity in changing historical circumstances. Many of these issues are still topics of debate and ongoing research; for instance, when did the definitive separation between the synagogues and the church occur? Many would argue that this separation occurred much later than previously believed and influences between the two groups continued well into the Christian era.

A renewed understanding of Jewish worship at the time of Jesus and his earlier disciples calls for a greater humility in what we know or can know about these early centuries. Firstly, much of what later centuries see as fixed is still at this point fluid and in a state of development. For instance, it has often been claimed that the Christian eucharistic prayers have as their direct origin Jewish table prayers. Yet, the earliest texts that we have come from nine hundred years after the ministry of Jesus. Therefore, we cannot claim to know what the texts of these prayers were like at the time of Jesus. At best, we can know the broad outline of a prayer of blessing that followed the end of a meal. However, we cannot argue with any certainty what the details of the prayer looked like or indeed if it was the only prayer in use. Indeed it would be mistaken to see meal prayers as already fixed at this point or attempting to see a direct connection between them and what Christians later call eucharistic prayers. Similar caution is required for any other prayer text.

As scholars have learnt more about the evolving state of Jewish worship in the period immediately before the destruction of the temple, they have also come to realise that the Jewish festivals attested to in the gospel accounts and celebrated by Jesus and his disciples, do not have the same form that are found in later rabbinical accounts. This is especially true of the Passover Seder. It seems well-nigh impossible to reconstruct how this Seder may have been celebrated in the first century CE and care is required in making any direct parallel between the event of the Last Supper and the rabbinic seder.

A greater attention to the variety of Christian and Jewish groups in these early centuries with their complex attitudes to each other helps to explain in a more satisfactory way why there seems to be differences in some of the gospel accounts. For instance, the issue of chronology in the Passion accounts. Some Christian communities remained attached to their traditional practices whereas others who came from different traditions may have seen these practices as examples of 'Judaising'. This affects the date of Easter, what the meaning of Easter is and the use or not of the Hebrew Bible in the liturgy itself. Some liturgies reflecting their communities maintain a strong Semitic flavour and others because of their origins show little of a Jewish connection.

Continuing attention by biblical scholars to the accounts of the Last Supper has enabled liturgists to understand Early Christian attitudes to the Jerusalem temple, its sacrificial worship and their own use of sacrificial metaphors. Some of these same scholars no longer see the Last Supper as an anti-temple act or the Last Supper and the temple sacrifice as opposing actions. Rightly, they ask if early Christians and especially Paul were so opposed to temple sacrifice, as has been argued by many interpreters, why did the centre of the Christian movement remain in Jerusalem. Many biblical scholars now reject the term 'the spiritualisation of sacrifice'. Rather they argue that what is happening in many Jewish groups is an extension of Exodus 19:6 or a 'sacrificialisation of the non-sacrificial worship' of various groups. There is a growing realisation that this too is divine service. Paul continues to use cultic language and describe worship as a sacrificial service. A similar critique could be made at drawing too great a contrast between the preaching of the prophets and the sacrifice of the temple.

As you leave this book aside, you may well reflect that the end is only a beginning and that is true! For further reading, you might well take up the work of another Irish liturgist, Liam Walsh, who published a book on the Eucharist in 2019.* The best single treatment of the history of the celebration of the Eucharist, with its theology, music and art, is still the work of the American Capuchin Edward Foley, and it has pictures!**

---

* Liam G. Walsh OP, *The Mass: Yesterday, Today … and Forever* (Dublin: Dominican Publications, 2019).

** Edward Foley, *From Age to Age: How Christians have celebrated the Eucharist,* (Collegeville, MN: The Liturgical Press, 2009). For further reading on early Christianity the standard treatment is now Andrew B. McGowan, *Ancient Christian Worship: Early Church Practices in Social, Historical and Theological Perspective* (Grand Rapids, MI: Baker Academic, 2016).

Endnotes

These notes are an editorial addition.

Readers of the reflections here in *Remember and Give Thanks* might like to note some related articles by Patrick McGoldrick:

'The Eucharistic Prayer' in *Understanding the Eucharist*, Patrick McGoldrick, ed. (Dublin: Gill and Macmillan, 1969), pp. 29–46.

'The Holy Spirit and the Eucharist', *Irish Theological Quarterly*, 50:1 (1983), pp. 48–66.

'Memorial' in *The New Dictionary of Theology*, Joseph A. Komonchak, Mary Collins, Dermot A. Lane, eds (Dublin: Gill and Macmillan, 1987), pp. 643–9.

'Orders, Sacrament of' in *The New Dictionary of Sacramental Worship*, Peter E. Fink SJ, ed. (Dublin: Gill and Macmillan, 1990), pp. 896–908.

'Liturgy: The Context of Patristic Exegesis' in *Scriptural Interpretation in the Fathers: Letter and Spirit*, Thomas Finan, Vincent Twomey, eds (Dublin: Four Courts Press, 1995), pp. 27–37.

'*Lex Orandi*: Memorial in the Eucharistic Prayers of the *Roman Missal*' in *Finding Voice to Give God Praise*, Kathleen Hughes, ed. (Collegeville, MN: Liturgical Press, 1998), pp. 128–38.

'The Gift of the Eucharist: A Reflection' in *Serving Liturgical Renewal*, Liam M. Tracey and Thomas R. Whelan, eds (Dublin: Veritas, 2015), pp. 143–51.

Chapter 1

[1] This chapter was given as a presentation at a day of recollection for the priests of the Diocese of Derry at the Carmelite Retreat Centre, Termonbacca, Derry on 11 December 2019. It was published in *The Furrow*, June 2020 and reprinted here with minor amendments by permission of the editor, Dr Pádraig Corkery.

[2] Thomas Merton, *The Seven Storey Mountain* (London: SPCK, 2015, SPCK classic, centenary edition), pp. 246–50.

[3] The Eucharistic Prayer as a source of understanding eucharist is seen in the paper given at the Maynooth Union Summer School in 1968: Patrick McGoldrick, 'The Eucharistic Prayer,' in *Understanding the Eucharist*, Patrick McGoldrick, ed. (Dublin: Gill and Macmillan, 1969), pp. 29–46.

[4] The Roman Canon was used in Rome from around the fifth century or earlier and became the sole Eucharistic prayer of the Roman Rite since the eleventh–twelfth century. After Vatican II, in the work of revision of the *Roman Missal*, the possibility of additional prayers was accepted. Three new prayers were introduced with the revised Order of Mass in 1968, making the Roman Canon Eucharistic Prayer I. Two more prayers on the theme of reconciliation were composed for the Holy Year of 1995. As well as these prayers, the third edition of the *Roman Missal* of 2010 contains four additional Eucharistic Prayers for use in Masses for Various Needs. In addition, three Eucharistic Prayers for Masses with Children were issued in 1975.

[5] Eucharist as God's gift is a frequent theme in these reflections. See Patrick McGoldrick, 'The Gift of the Eucharist: A Reflection,' *Serving Liturgical Renewal*, Liam M. Tracey and Thomas R. Whelan, eds (Dublin: Veritas, 2015), pp. 143–51.

Chapter 2

[6] Patristic sources offer an understanding of liturgy today. See Patrick McGoldrick, 'Liturgy: The Context of Patristic Exegesis,' *Scriptural Interpretation in the Fathers: Letter and Spirit*, Thomas Finan and Vincent Twomey, eds (Dublin: Four Courts Press, 1995), pp. 27–37. Having written his doctoral thesis on St Augustine's teaching of the holiness of the Church, Patrick McGoldrick retained his interest in Augustine throughout his life and several references to Augustine are to be found in this collection of reflections on eucharist.

Augustine, honoured as a Doctor of the Church of the West, was a prolific writer. In 1990 New City Press, New York, in conjunction with the

Augustinian Heritage Institute, founded by John E. Rotelle OSA, began the project of publishing the complete 132 works of Augustine in modern English. To date, forty-four of the forty-nine volumes have been published as *The Works of Saint Augustine: A Translation for the 21st Century.*

[7] Augustine, *City of God*, 10:5. The classic formula, 'sacrament as the outward and visible sign of inward and invisible grace' goes back to the fifth-century theologian.

Chapter 3

[8] The Eucharistic Prayer is 'the centre and high point' of the celebration of eucharist (*General Instruction of the Roman Missal*, 78). Known as the *anaphora* or offering in the Eastern Churches, its very name reflects its element of thanksgiving. In the institution narrative and consecration, 'by means of words and actions of Christ, that sacrifice is effected which Christ himself instituted during the Last Supper, when he offered his body and blood under the species of bread and wine, gave them to the apostles to eat and drink, and leaving with the latter the command to perpetuate this same mystery' (*GIRM*, 79, d). The main elements of the Eucharistic Prayer are thanksgiving, acclamation, *epiclesis* (invocation of the Holy Spirit), institution narrative and consecration, *anamnesis* (memorial), oblation (offering), intercessions and doxology (the concluding expression of God's glory).

[9] Augustine, *City of God*, 10:6: 'This wholly redeemed city, the assembly and society of the saints, is offered to God as a universal sacrifice by the high priest who in the form of a slave went so far as to offer himself for us in his Passion, to make us the Body of so great a head ... Such is the sacrifice of Christians: "we who are many are one Body in Christ." The Church continues to reproduce this sacrifice in the sacrament of the altar so well known to believers wherein it is evident to them that in what she offers she herself is offered.' See *Catechism of the Catholic Church*, 1372.

Chapter 6

[10] These words are taken from Vatican II, Decree on the Ministry and Life of Priests, *Presbyterorum Ordinis*, 5, promulgated on 7 December 1965 as the Council ended. The words are quoted on p. 48 of an article by Patrick McGoldrick, 'The Holy Spirit and the Eucharist', *Irish Theological Quarterly*, 50:1 (1983), pp. 48–66.

Chapter 8

[11] In the year 304, in Abitina, a town in present-day Tunisia, forty-nine Christians were arrested for illegal assembly; for gathering in the house of Octavius Felix for Sunday eucharist with Saturninus, the priest. At their trial, Emeritus, a reader, said, *sine dominico non possumus* ('without Sunday we cannot live'). Sentenced to death, they died 'martyrs for Sunday'.

Chapter 9

[12] Jerome, *Commentary on the Book of Isaiah, Prologue*. St Jerome wrote, 'Ignorance of the Scriptures is ignorance of Christ,' a statement often quoted, including Vatican II, Constitution on Divine Revelation, *Dei Verbum*, 25.

[13] Augustine, *Seven Questions concerning the Heptateuch*, 2, 73. Another statement also often quoted, including Vatican II, Constitution on Divine Revelation, *Dei Verbum*, 16.

Chapter 14

[14] See Augustine, *Sermon* 229A, where he speaks of bread and wine filling the belly but when consecrated to be the Body and Blood of Christ and eaten, the spirit is nourished. In a homily on the Solemnity of the Body and Blood of our Lord, June 2011, Pope Benedict XVI said, 'Therefore whereas food for the body is assimilated by our organism and contributes to nourishing it, in the case of the eucharist it is a different Bread: it is not we who assimilate it but it assimilates us in itself, so that we become conformed to Jesus Christ, a member of his Body, one with him.'

[15] Augustine, *Sermon* 272. Preaching on Pentecost Sunday, early fifth century, to those baptised at Easter, Augustine reminded them that as members of the body of Christ, 'it is the mystery meaning you that has been placed on the Lord's table; what you receive is the mystery that means you. It is to what you are that you reply Amen, and by so replying you express your assent. What you hear, you see, is the body of Christ, and you answer, Amen. So be a member of the body of Christ, in order that Amen be true.' In an Easter Sunday sermon (227), addressing the newly baptised, he summed this up in a few words: 'you are yourselves what you receive.'

Chapter 15

[16] Thomas Merton, *Conjectures of a Guilty Bystander* (Garden City NY: Doubleday, 1966), pp. 140–2. 'Now that I realise what we all are,' at the corner of Fourth and Walnut Streets, Louisville, on 18 May 1958.

Chapter 16

17 Augustine, *Letter to Proba* (Letter 130). In the year 412, as Bishop of Hippo, Augustine writes to Proba on prayer, 'God wants our desire to be exercised in prayer, thus enabling us to grasp what he is preparing to give ... We shall have the greater capacity to receive it, the more trustfully we believe, the more firmly we hope, the more ardently we desire. So we pray always with unfailing desire in that faith, hope and charity.' Excerpts from the letter are given as the second reading in the Office of Readings, 29th Week in Ordinary Time, Sunday to Friday.

Chapter 18

18 Augustine, *Commentary on Psalm 98:5,* says, 'Let no one eat Christ's flesh, except he first adore it.' This is cited by St Thomas Aquinas, *Summa Theologica,* III, 80, q. 7 ad. 2 (= *PL* 37, 559).